Notes from the Rehearsal Room

Notes from the Rehearsal Room

A Director's Process

Nancy Meckler

methuen | drama

LONDON · NEW YORK · OXFORD · NEW DELHI · SYDNEY

METHUEN DRAMA
Bloomsbury Publishing Plc
50 Bedford Square, London, WC1B 3DP, UK
1385 Broadway, New York, NY 10018, USA
29 Earlsfort Terrace, Dublin 2, Ireland

BLOOMSBURY, METHUEN DRAMA and the Methuen Drama logo are trademarks
of Bloomsbury Publishing Plc

First published in Great Britain 2023

Some names have been changed to protect individuals' privacy.

Cover image: L-R: Claire Benedict, Peter Hamilton-Dyer,
Nancy Meckler (© Sarah Ainslie)

A catalogue record for this book is available from the British Library.

A catalog record for this book is available from the Library of Congress.

ISBN: HB: 978-1-3502-8221-6
       PB: 978-1-3502-8220-9
       ePDF: 978-1-3502-8223-0
       eBook: 978-1-3502-8222-3

Series: Theatre Makers

Typeset by RefineCatch Limited, Bungay, Suffolk

To find out more about our authors and books visit www.bloomsbury.com
and sign up for our newsletters.

*For all the actors with whom I have
shared the journey*

CONTENTS

Introduction

Directing a play involves taking words off a page and bringing them to a place where they exist physically in time and space, where others can see, hear and feel them.

Actors are fortunate. In their working lives they will encounter any number of directors and their individual ways of working, whereas we theatre directors rarely have that opportunity. Often the tools and techniques of our trade are learned haphazardly through reading, workshops and early forays into acting.

For me, above all, making theatre feeds a desire to express what it means to be fully human. In life so often we repress or hide our emotions, our needs, our aspirations. But when we watch theatre, film or television drama we satisfy a hunger for experience. As spectators we can identify what matters to us. We can explore possible experience. We can learn about extremes of human behaviour, we can see enacted the kinds of open, frank, frightening conversations which may be infrequent in our daily lives. At best we come to feel and care about characters. When we care about what happens to them, to hope for their success or survival, we make an emotional connection. As we watch a play, it might be said that the actors are expressing emotions for us, feelings we might find too intense in real life. And I do not hesitate to include comedy in this realm. Comedy might lighten our hearts, but its roots are deeply serious.

Our sense of mortality is always present somewhere in our minds, but when we create I believe we become most fully alive.

How do we get to this point of a piece of art existing off the page? Of connecting actors and the audience with each other and with the essence of the play?

A bit about me

Before the age of 10 I was making theatre. I had become obsessed with creating stories, gathering neighbourhood kids together to 'make a show' which we would then perform for any audience we could find. Given that television was new then, it is unlikely that I would have seen theatre of any kind, although I do remember at the age of 5 attending a recital at the local dance school. From that moment I was smitten with the idea of performance. Which led to my intense passion for acting, followed years later by an involvement in all areas of theatre and finally into directing.

I was a drama major from 1958 to 1963 at Antioch College, a liberal arts university in America's Midwest with a small theatre department. This meant that we few students had plenty of opportunities to make theatre and take on creative roles. Part of my studies was a course in Basic Directing and I subsequently went on to direct a few student productions, but at that time woman theatre directors were so rare that it would never have occurred to me as a possible career. All our drama professors were men; each summer we had professional directors visiting from New York City and they too were men. There were simply no role models which would inspire women to become directors.

As my driving passion since childhood was to one day become an actor, a lack of opportunities for women in directing was not a problem. And I pursued acting by persistently auditioning for roles in college productions. However, to my dismay, I was rarely cast in the sought-after summer season which included professional actors. The disappointment was huge. My hunger for a life in the theatre meant a longing to be in a rehearsal room, as close as possible to the process. But it soon became apparent that the only areas open to me were in costumes, lighting or stage management.

Stage management did not feel particularly creative but it had its attractions. I would be at the director's side, taking down blocking, running the rehearsal room and being closely involved with every area of production. This was my route into the process, and I hungrily took the option. I eventually saw there was a danger in becoming too valuable as a stage manager and I was not keen to be stuck in that role. Little did I know that one day when I began directing, those years working in stage management would serve as a virtual apprenticeship.

After university and an internship at Washington DC's Arena Stage, I returned to my pursuit of acting, attending classes at the HB (Herbert Berghof) Studios in New York. Those classes with several truly inspiring teachers, including Bill Hickey and Aaron Frankel, introduced me to the basic tenets of acting and were to be invaluable in the future. To this day I use many exercises first encountered there.

Fruitless attempts to find acting work in the cattle call auditions of New York were followed by a year studying classical acting in the UK at the London Academy of Music and Dramatic Art (LAMDA). During that year of study I gradually and painfully came to realize that acting was not right for me. I loved theatre, I wanted to be a part of it, but no longer as a performer.

I was fortunate to discover that my previous forays into directing at university meant I could offer my services as assistant director to alternative theatre companies which were springing up in New York and London. These companies were often unfunded and therefore open and welcoming to young, dedicated, idealistic theatre makers. Ellen Stewart's La MaMa Experimental Theatre Club became an umbrella for many such companies and I was able to join La MaMa Plexus in New York as an assistant director.

In 1968 I came to live in the UK during a period now referred to as the second wave of feminism, when the phrase 'women's libbers' was born. Women's groups and women's theatre companies were springing up and although I never joined a particular group, I was aware of this exciting activity full of passion and adventurous intent. Looking back, feminism may not have been foremost in my conscious mind as I was pursing a singular passion – to have a creative life in the theatre. At that time Wherehouse La MaMa, an offshoot of the New York La MaMa, was starting up and I joined them as a directing assistant.

Within a year a small breakaway company, Freehold, evolved and I became their director. Our great fringe success at the 1969 Edinburgh Festival with a version of Sophocles' *Antigone* devised by the company and Peter Hulton, was quickly followed by a dazzling sequence of events. We were invited by the Akademie der Kunste to open their theatre festival in Berlin and later that year the British Council presented us at BITEF (Belgrade International Theatre Festival) and the Venice Biennale. This whirlwind response led to us becoming one of the first fringe theatre groups to receive Arts Council funding, so finally we could pay a weekly wage.

The Freehold company survived barely four years (1968–73), partly because I had married and taken time out to have a baby. This meant having to bring in visiting directors for several productions, always difficult when a company has a strong history and work ethic. Also, our Arts Council funding required lengthy tours which were simply not compatible with having a small child.

In the following years my work has taken me into many spheres: new writing, directing feature films, and working in ballet as a director and a dramaturg. For twenty-two years I led an Arts Council touring company, Shared Experience Theatre. And I have directed many Shakespeare productions for the Royal Shakespeare Company and Shakespeare's Globe.

A woman in theatre

Women's lives and women's issues may not have been a conscious commitment and yet, in every working opportunity, I was drawn to women playwrights and intuitively chose women's stories. My work for Freehold began by exploring a women's theme: a study for the witches in *Macbeth*. Later projects were the deconstructed version of Sophocles' *Antigone* and Webster's *The Duchess of Malfi*. Add to this our production of *The Successful Life of Three* by Maria Irene Fornes, an American playwright, and my inclination was evident.

When asked whether being a woman has ever held me back as a theatre director, I can cite many instances when being a woman and a mother of two has meant turning down work away from home, which might otherwise have led to a smooth path up the proverbial career ladder. And I can cite numerous occasions of being ignored or rejected when there was most likely an unconscious bias against women. But when I spent over twenty years as the artistic director of Shared Experience Theatre, we made a consistent effort to employ women in every sphere. In the late 1990s Polly Teale became my directing associate and eventually my co-artistic director. Together we sought the talents of women designers, writers, movement directors, production managers, senior staff and board members. As a general rule I find women are particularly open to collaboration and this was a deeply collaborative environment. We certainly did not exclude men. One crucial member of our creative team was composer Peter Salem, who created inspiring and wide-ranging scores for so many of our productions including *War and Peace*, co-produced with the National Theatre in 1996.

Diversity

As I write this book, we in the theatre are experiencing an important sea change in our commitment to addressing diversity in all areas of production. The Black Lives Matter movement, begun circa 2014, has led to heightened awareness of diversity shortcomings in our profession. When I began as artistic director of Shared Experience Theatre in 1989, my intention was to open doors whenever possible to actors, writers, assistants and technical people of colour. Thereafter we made efforts to continue in this vein; certainly our expressionistic productions encouraged us towards more open casting. Subsequently in my freelance career I have worked with casting directors committed to opening the field as widely as possible.

It hugely bothers me that the pool of people from diverse backgrounds trained in backstage and technical skills is so limited. There are efforts made now by the National Theatre and producers to introduce people at a very young age to those skills and opportunities, and sixth form colleges have begun offering training in technical skills. Hopefully this will open the way to many who would never have considered a behind-the-scenes life in the arts.

Physical theatre

People reading this book might expect me to deal with the many years I have spent working in physical theatre. Shared Experience Theatre was certainly devoted to that realm and we created extra-long rehearsal periods so that we could train actors physically and prepare them for rehearsals requiring physical exploration and physical expression. In fact our working credo was a commitment to expressionism: work that explores the hidden feelings, thoughts, dreams and aspirations of its characters through physical expression. To give an example: when Anna in *Anna Karenina* became addicted to morphine, we created a movement sequence to express the immediate physical effect each time she sipped the drug. Such movement sequences underpinned by a sound score were virtually bordering on dance, but in this case performed by an actor. These moments were a creative collaboration between the actor, the director and our movement director, the remarkable Liz Ranken. Liz is a theatre artist working in dance and theatre with performers of diverse abilities. She was able to craft a sequence with an actor through improvisation, using their first nonverbal instincts as her starting point. Because movement work in our company was initiated from actor impulses, it had an immediacy and an honesty which was engaging and often deeply moving.

In the late 1980s when I met director and teacher Mladen Materic at the Edinburgh Festival, I discovered his extensive method of physical exercises which provided a clear and precise way for introducing physical exploration to a rehearsal room. We invited him to Shared Experience for workshops, where I learned a new and exciting vocabulary.

In sharing my process I plan to touch only briefly on this physical work. Physical exercises need to be experienced or at least observed; describing them tends to be unsatisfactory and indeed can be easily misunderstood. I have decided to limit this book to a process which can be communicated through the written word. Most importantly, I want to emphasize that these written exercises are the keystones I would use in every rehearsal room, whether the work is traditional or 'physical'. In fact, I have often brought them into use when working with dancers on their acting in narrative ballet.

Why this book?

My generation of theatre directors, emerging in the 1960s and 1970s rarely had any formal training and often came to directing through their time at university. As a result there were probably as many ways to direct plays as there were directors.

Nowadays there are courses and books on directing. In my experience, reading about exercises and then trying them out is only occasionally successful. But when it is, those few exercises can become a solid and invaluable base for the work. Inevitably these exercises morph into something else as you discover how they work and how they work for you.

In this book I am offering up some of the tools I use when bringing a play to life. Many of these are my own invention, discovered through trial and error. For example, I have never studied improvisation, but gradually have developed a technique for using it in the rehearsal room. I came to believe that starting rehearsals by sharing basic starting points and vocabulary with the company lays down a common understanding of priorities and prepares the ground for true ensemble playing.

Finally, as I believe that we learn best by doing, rather than by watching or having things explained to us, it is my hope that some of these tools will come across as suggestions, which can spark off ideas. You might try them out, or better yet, they might encourage you to invent your own. However you use them, I hope you find what follows stimulating and even useful.

1

Preparation

With any play I am asked to direct I am looking for a gut response, a feeling that it touches me in some way. That there is something in the play that I can engage with passionately, an essence which I have a real desire to share with an audience. This is not always obvious, and I might have to dig to find that special connection.

Film director Jim Sheridan, who had directed Daniel Day Lewis so brilliantly in *My Left Foot*, was advising me. It was 1993 and I was about to direct my first feature film *Sister My Sister* (based on Wendy Kesselman's fine stage play *My Sister in This House* which I had directed for Monstrous Regiment). Sheridan and I sat in a Vietnamese restaurant off Shaftesbury Avenue as he posed a question: 'Can you say what the film is about in one sentence?' I was startled by this challenge coming from a film director. It was a really valuable exercise easily applied to theatre, and is one I always revisit. I have learned that if I cannot find that one sentence, then there is a problem, either with me or with the script.

My search to find the one sentence that tells us what the play is about is closely aligned with my passion for telling the story with clarity. Once we know what it is about, can the story take us on a journey? How clear is the story telling? Does every moment in the play, every physical detail of set and lighting, every sound contribute to that journey? For me it is not enough for a theatre piece to be beautiful or entertaining, it also has to 'move' us, open up our thinking, give us new or true experience.

The protagonist

Protagonist from the Greek:

protos: first in importance
agonistes: actor

I believe that drama requires a protagonist, a main character with strong needs which are difficult to satisfy or achieve. We engage with the story when we recognize this character's desires, and we are concerned because the outcome is unpredictable. How will they fare? Will they succeed or fail? Will they surmount difficulties on the way to their goal or will they be destroyed by the attempt? Once the protagonist has been identified it should be possible to describe the story in one sentence.

A proviso: In rare instances the protagonist can be several characters, as in Chekhov's *The Three Sisters*, where we follow three journeys in time simultaneously.

To sum up: It is essential to develop a sentence that includes a protagonist with a huge need, faced with challenging obstacles and a questionable outcome. Ideally the solution to this one-sentence challenge goes beyond coming up with a one-word theme. Longish sentences are allowed!

Examples

Romeo and Juliet by William Shakespeare
Two young lovers from warring families pursue love in danger to their lives.
or
Two families at war with each other are blinded by their need to dominate and end up destroying those dearest to them.

Death of a Salesman by Arthur Miller
Willy Loman, an older man who has pursued the American
Dream of recognition and success in the world, comes to see
his life as a failure and is grasping for respect and self-belief as
he loses his grip on reality.

Top Girls by Caryl Churchill
Women determined to have an adventurous, totally fulfilled
life struggle to survive in a world which traditionally restricts
them in every way.

A Midsummer Night's Dream by William Shakespeare
(This example relates to my Royal Shakespeare Company
(RSC) production of 2011. Given that the play has three sets
of characters and three interweaving storylines, the sentence is
unsurprisingly complex.)
Characters locked into a struggle for dominance and freedom
go to sleep and enter a dream world in which their fears and
sexual desires are unleashed, resulting in huge confusion, and
a final restoration to love and forgiveness.

The impossible sentence

When I cannot form the essential single sentence which says
what the play is about, I know there is a problem. A few years
back I was working on Martin Sherman's play *Onassis* about
a world-famous powerful figure, but found I could not craft
the single sentence that told his story. As it was proving so
difficult, it became apparent that exceptional and event-filled
life stories do not necessarily suggest a dramatic through line.
And it explains why so many films we call biopics fail for the
same reason. They are always somewhat interesting, but they
lack a driving force. *Onassis* was a challenge for me to find the
central need or quest from the myriad of biographical detail
and events in this provocative play. A starting point: a ruthless,
wealthy and powerful man does not believe the rules of society

apply to him, but when his son is murdered the gods work their revenge.

Working with writers

Working on new material with a writer can be a thrilling experience. Reading a play, having a positive gut response to it, then finding a theatre that wants to produce it – what an opportunity. Whereas every director will find their own way of working with a writer, here are a few guidelines which I have evolved over time.

New play – new writer

Try to establish early on what the play is about. Can the writer put it into one sentence or come up with a major theme? What does the play want to say? Does it aspire to achieve something vis-à-vis an audience?

This question can be puzzling for any writer, or they might feel resistant to the idea of reducing their play to something so basic. As the writer/director relationship is particularly sensitive, I try to talk this through without being too opinionated or forceful. After all, I too need to know the answer to this question. And if the play is trying to deal with several themes, it may be difficult to find a through line of action.

Feeling each other out: Dennis Potter

I had an unusual working experience when meeting the writer Dennis Potter to discuss his play *Sufficient Carbohydrate*. This was 1983 and Potter was now a celebrated writer, having created several extremely popular pieces for television, notably *Pennies from Heaven* and *Blue Remembered Hills*. *Sufficient Carbohydrate* was the only play he had written specifically for the stage and I was engaged by Hampstead Theatre to direct it. Presciently, Potter's play dealt with the harm we were doing to our food supply due to the demands of big business.

We met for the first time at his agent's office. Potter was combative, contradicting almost everything I had to offer, criticizing my questions as if they were foolish and unintelligent. This was alarming. After 20 minutes I took the bull by the horns and offered to step down as it was clear I was not the right person to direct his play. But Potter immediately rejected this, insisting 'Oh no, we are just feeling each other out'. He wanted a truthful and no-holds-barred conversation. I was surprised, thrown, and somewhat delighted. Needless to say, this was not a typical first meeting with a writer. But it gave me a sense of Dennis Potter and gave me licence to be open and honest with him.

Potter was already very ill with severe arthritis and psoriasis and therefore unable to attend rehearsals beyond the first reading. A few weeks into rehearsal I rang him to share my concerns that one of the scenes felt increasingly like a soap opera. The actors were uncomfortable as they felt they were veering toward melodrama. Dennis then explained that in fact he was purposely using the soap opera form in order to make serious points precisely because he had something important to say. He had written this play as a warning, and he believed the commercial soap opera form would make the material more palatable to an audience. They would be more likely to listen, hear, and perhaps consider his message. I was full of admiration for Potter's thinking and glad to share it with the actors, who were reassured.

Readings: Pros and cons

Let's assume that you would not have been attracted to this play nor pursued a production unless you had felt engaged by its central core/drive. An essence that made you want to turn the page to see what would happen next. Perhaps the next step was to request a reading. Many theatres are keen for this, as it helps them decide whether or not to embark on a production.

It's worth bearing in mind that the likelihood of accurate casting for the reading is rare and frankly that can be confusing. Before we have an audience we read the play aloud, perhaps with a few hours' rehearsal. Others are then invited to listen as we read it through. Frankly, I am often none the wiser and I know some writers who would feel the same. In all probability I am distracted by so many unfamiliar faces and new personalities in the space. And, if the actors are not right for their roles, it is always a major distraction.

But it is also true that writers can get real knowledge and stimulus from a reading. Despite inaccurate casting, hearing their words spoken aloud for the first time is a valuable experience. Indeed an extended rehearsal, over several days, can lead to a promising reading which may give a producing theatre confidence to proceed with the project.

Working on the script before rehearsal

In the weeks before rehearsal of the actual production, I would ideally meet with the playwright several times. This can be part of the casting process. Having the writer in casting sessions can be a great entrée into the play as I learn so much from the writer's preferences. As the writer joins auditions and then comments on why actors are right or wrong for the parts, I come closer to understanding the characters and the writer's intentions.

In early meetings I would also flag up any areas which are confusing or need more development. Often when I question whether a scene or section is working, whether it takes the story forward, the writer will defend the scene adamantly. The writer might explain in depth what is happening, but if I cannot see it yet in the writing, I may question whether their intentions are coming through. Often, in fact, I find myself wondering if the writer is defending a scene they *wish* they had written. And I will then urge them to express their ideas more fully in the writing.

In the same vein, there are instances when a character is underwritten and needs more development on the page. The writer knows the characters so well that they can easily assume they have fully written the role. At these moments, the director is playing the part of the first audience – an audience that needs a way in, more clues or information.

Over the years, I have been supported by good advice about working on new writing from that fine theatre director Michael Rudman. When urging a writer in a new direction or towards solving a particular problem, Rudman suggests this: 'Have a think about it.' This approach keeps your relationship open. It means you are not locked in a battle that must be won in the moment by either party. And it gives the writer a chance to go away, absorb the challenge, think it through, and respond in a way that is truthful to their writing.

A warning

How tempting to be in a situation where all your suggestions are easily accepted by the writer and promptly put into practice. This can feel gratifying. But it can be dangerous. You are not the writer, and a writer who writes to order is merely trying to please. The best collaboration is one in which both sides are heard, but the writer feels able to consider, mull, and work with your ideas without sacrificing the core of the writing.

Needless to say, the writer may reject every single one of your suggestions. It is an understatement to say this can be deeply frustrating. At the very least, one hopes for a fruitful discussion. But this might not be possible. If the producer or company dramaturg is around, they can play a vital role, either by supporting you privately in hearing and discussing your ideas, or perhaps holding a meeting about the play with you and the writer present.

Discovering the secret play

We directors often find ourselves working on new material which we think needs improvement. But, no matter how hard we try, we are not always able to achieve that. This means that as we direct the play, we are looking for ways to hide the play's weaknesses, disguise its faults, with a greater or lesser degree of success.

But there is another possibility for the director. This is the occasion when we root out the hidden, unconscious play – in effect, the play which the writer has no conscious idea they have written. Writing is a mysterious art, much of it coming from the unconscious, and a hidden play just might be embedded in the writing – waiting there to be rooted out, emphasized and developed.

Rewrites – a conundrum

Many writers write instinctively; they say the play just comes to them, that it flows out from some mysterious place. And these writers may have a problem with rewriting. They are simply at a loss to improve or adjust their work. If a writer repeatedly brings in rewrites which you feel are not an improvement, of course you will be less inclined to ask for changes.

On the other hand, I find many writers are comfortable when it comes to adding new material. Working with a new writer is a learning process for both of us.

Pam Gems

In 1972 the inimitable Pam Gems entered my life. Pam, mother of four growing children, was in her late forties and had only recently begun writing plays. We met when my husband David Aukin produced her first play *Betty's Wonderful Christmas* in a season of new work at the tiny Cockpit Theatre off Lisson

Grove. Several years later in 1975 Pam sent me a one-act called *The Project*.

My interest in this play led to a meeting with Pam and Verity Bargate, then artistic director of the Soho Poly, a tiny lunchtime theatre in a basement on Riding House Street in London's West End. Verity can only be described as a major force, running the theatre on her own at this point, producing new and little-known work on a shoestring, championing countless new writers. I sat opposite these two formidable women and explained to them that as I was pregnant I was therefore unable to direct *The Project* for their dates. I would be breastfeeding and had found it definitely needed my full commitment. To this day I marvel at their response. They did not hesitate, but insisted that they would wait until I was ready to work.

There were two women and one man in the piece. As the rehearsal date approached it proved incredibly difficult to find an actor willing to play the male character in this female-dominated play. Thankfully, and literally at the last minute, the brilliant David Schofield accepted the part. He was a great company member, and we played to sell-out houses. In the following year Schofield created his groundbreaking performance as John Merrick, the Elephant Man, in Bernard Pomerance's remarkable play.

Hard to believe that Pam Gems was 51 when she wrote *Dusa, Fish, Stas and Vi*, a play which dug into and laid open the emotional lives of a younger generation of women – women in their mid-twenties who were navigating the tricky environment of changing attitudes to sex, marriage and patriarchy. Originally produced at the Edinburgh Festival with the title *Dead Fish*, a second production was planned at Hampstead Theatre Club, and I was invited to direct it under its new name.

Many short plays of Gems's had previously been produced on the fringe and brought her into contact with a younger generation of women. She was intrigued by their concerns, their problems, their choices. Opening at a difficult time of year in the weeks before Christmas 1976, *Dusa, Fish, Stas and*

Vi was an unexpected and resounding success, going on to a West End run at the Mayfair Theatre and winning a best actress award at the SWET (now Olivier) Awards for Alison Fiske, dazzling in the lead role of Fish. Somehow Pam Gems had opened a door to a female world that people were hungry to learn about.

Later Pam and I worked together on her adaptations of Chekhov's *Uncle Vanya* and *The Cherry Orchard*. The brilliant and gracious Russian-born Tanya Alexander provided our literal translation and one of my fondest memories is the three of us poring over Chekhov's text, prising out his meaning and discovering his inspiring subtlety.

Revivals

I have had the great good fortune to direct revivals by several established writers including Sam Shepard, Harold Pinter and Edward Albee. These are all male writers, which gives me pause to wonder at how difficult it has been for women to attain real, established recognition as playwrights. And looking back, I realize how extraordinary it was to be treated as an equal by these men in a profession where women were struggling for recognition.

How fortuitous that these writers were keen to talk with me about 'what I was thinking' or 'wanted to say' with their play. This was reassuring and always provided insight.

Edward Albee

I met Edward Albee in New York in 1978 when I was about to direct his classic *Who's Afraid of Virginia Woolf?* for the National Theatre. In fact this was a historic moment, as I was to be the first woman to direct a play there, invited by Michael Rudman, who was running the Lyttleton Theatre at the National. He had supported me since first seeing my work for Freehold in the late 1960s.

I was pleased to be meeting Albee, who was happy to share what he wanted to say, what he was thinking about. He imparted that he had been mostly dissatisfied with productions of *Who's Afraid of Virginia Woolf?* because he thought the play should be an equal battle between his two main characters, Martha and George. He envisioned them as major contenders in a three-round heavyweight battle. But he was usually disappointed, because Martha often came across as a tormentor and George, her husband, as the victim. He urged me to address this and balance their effect on each other. Albee was saying that he wanted an equal battle.

I returned to London hoping to carry out Albee's intentions. But in performance I came to suspect that although Martha showed real and touching vulnerability in the final scene, the audience was always going to see her as the gorgon and George as the long-suffering husband. Was this perhaps an instance of the writer describing the play he wished he had written rather than the one he *had* written?

Albee came to watch one of our last run-throughs and he gave a list of written notes. We met the next day to review them, and he had questioned why Martha was shouting furiously at one point. I opened the script and pointed to his stage direction, which said something like: *Martha shouts furiously*. Albee took out his rather elegant fountain pen and calmly crossed out the stage direction, saying: 'That was me thirty years ago.'

Of course it was a terrific lesson, and I now agree with so many directors who ask the actors to scrub out any stage directions before they study the script. They can be prescriptive in the wrong way and modern playwrights are less likely to use them.

Sam Shepard

Icarus' Mother by Sam Shepard is a short, obscure play which I discovered in a collection of Shepard's early works. Although it was a puzzling piece, I had always been drawn to his writing, which I found mysterious and intriguing. In the early 1970s Shepard was spending the winter months in London and we were able to meet. He gave me permission to direct a fringe production of the play to be performed by my company Freehold.

I came across an introduction to *Icarus' Mother* written by its first director, Michael Smith. He had directed the play in 1965 and felt that he only managed to confuse his actors as he grappled unsuccessfully with its meaning. Happily for me, Shepard was open to talking about the piece, offering to explain what he was thinking when he wrote it. Basically the play is about a fear of flying. At that time Shepard's refusal to travel by air was widely known – pretty amusing when one remembers that years later (1983) he played Chuck Yeager in *The Right Stuff*, a film about the test pilot who flew the plane that broke the sound barrier.

Shepard's simple clue for me – 'a fear of flying' – was a gift. It hinted at the inner lives of the characters and explained their erratic and sometimes surreal behaviour. With Freehold I had been exploring expressionism. I can briefly describe expressionism as digging into the unseen thoughts, desires and fears of characters and expressing them in sound and movement or in non-naturalistic behaviour. Because of this work, we were ready for this insight from the writer. It released us into a fruitful and satisfying rehearsal period with Shepard occasionally in attendance and we performed it at the Roxy, a converted garage in London's Kentish Town. Shepard loved the rehearsals and the production, which led to me directing many works by him. My production of his play *Action* appeared first at the Royal Court Theatre Upstairs (1972) and later at the American Place Theater in New York.

In the following years I directed several Shepard plays: *Buried Child, True West,* and premieres of *The Curse of the Starving Class, Killer's Head* and his final play, *A Particle of Dread: Oedipus Variations*. For me Shepard's work is resonant, full of poetry, humanity and love. Sam could be a demanding taskmaster and his friendship and respect for me as a director is something I shall always cherish. I consider it a real a privilege to have had that ongoing relationship and to be associated with the man and his work.

Harold Pinter

It may come as a surprise that Harold Pinter circa 1968, after his huge successes with *The Birthday Party* and *The Homecoming*, was making dedicated efforts to follow the work of alternative theatre companies. My company, Freehold, were performing our deconstructed version of Sophocles' *Antigone* at Oval House, a youth centre in Kennington. Oval House was certainly off-West End and it had become host to many fringe theatre companies, giving us free space to rehearse and perform. Fortunately *Time Out* magazine, having just emerged, provided a source of unpaid publicity.

To our awe and delight, Harold Pinter and Vivien Merchant, then his wife, came to Kennington to see our show. Clearly he was interested in new work and was making serious efforts to seek it out. I wrote to Pinter asking if he might write something for us. Although he did not answer personally, we were impressed when an assistant sent an immediate reply politely explaining that Mr Pinter admired our work but did not have anything he felt he could offer.

As time went by, Pinter continued to follow my work, often sending a congratulatory note. When we were about to rehearse *The Birthday Party* for a Shared Experience tour, being his usual generous self, he offered to send me a letter he had written to its first director, Peter Wood, describing his understanding of the characters of Goldberg and McCann. The letter dealt with them as Establishment figures, identifying them as 'socio-religious mobsters' representing family and religion. Although I felt privileged to be given the letter, to this day I am not sure it was a help to have this puzzling and intriguing play demystified. It is always problematic when you ask actors to play a concept. Pinter's writing is so powerful and intense that I think I would rather the cast and I had found our own route through it.

Pinter was, as ever, supportive throughout the process, even travelling to the Sherman Theatre Studio in Cardiff to watch an evening performance, later taking the whole company out for a Chinese meal. He was genuinely pleased with the production. Turning to Peter Whitman playing Goldberg, he gave him a new line as he exited into the hallway when he was to compliment Meg on the beauty of her staircase. To this day I feel moved by Pinter's commitment to a touring production with no stars and no West End future. Not many writers of his stature would have been so generous. Perhaps we reminded him of his early years as a jobbing actor playing in regional theatres, having to live frugally and find acceptable digs in a new boarding house each week.

Premieres

With a new play I do feel committed to discovering the playwright's vision and serving it. So having the writer in the room can be helpful, but it can also be distracting. This is their baby. Do they trust me? Am I going to bring out the best in their work or am I distorting it? Have I cast it adequately and am I in line with the writer's taste? It is hard to avoid these questions popping into one's mind.

Ideally – and this is what I put to the writer – I would like them to be in rehearsal for the first week as we begin to investigate the play and explore its themes and characters. After each day's rehearsal I can connect with them about how things are going. For the next weeks I would like the writer to leave us to it, dropping in for short bursts, and then returning for a stagger-through in the penultimate week. From then on I would expect them to be around quite a bit as we do more run-throughs followed by notes.

Although it is rare to have the writer continually present, I have occasionally worked with writers where this was possible and supportive. When he was available, Sam Shepard wanted to be in rehearsal continuously. So does Martin Sherman, best known for his internationally famous play, *Bent*. Exceptionally, having these writers present was not a distraction. They gave a sense that they were in the room to support the work and be of help. They were fascinated by the process of rehearsal and were not judging results. It needs to be said that this was rare. In so many cases I have had a writer in the room who was mostly anxious and judgemental. Of course it can be frustrating for a writer to watch actors struggling to find their way into character and situation when to the writer it seems so obviously clear. Perfectly understandable, but not conducive to a relaxed atmosphere.

Devising

My early experiences of developing a script in continual collaboration with a writer were difficult and so unsatisfactory that I finally resolved 'Never again'. In the 1970s when I was running Freehold, writer Roy Kift and I had rehearsed, performed and toured his play *Mary, Mary*. Roy was present in many rehearsals and made adjustments as rehearsals progressed. All in all it was a satisfying creative journey.

Our next project was to create a theatre piece exploring the first five books of the Bible. As we began, Roy presented us with a working theme. Looking back at those lengthy rehearsals, I can see that we were swimming in deep water, trying to devise work without any tools or guidance for the devising process. It's worth mentioning that this was the 1970s, and we were passionate about breaking boundaries, working instinctively, and exploring outside the rules of how things should be done – definitely reinventing the wheel.

The company would explore the material, improvising physically and verbally. Roy would go home and write up scenes. On his return the entire company would have in-depth, democratic conversations as we discussed the writing and what it was saying or trying to say. As democratic process was revered and deemed essential, everyone had a say. We spent agonizing months on this piece and finally managed to put something together which we took on tour. But for me the final product was unsatisfactory. I now understand that facing the writer each time he brought in material with so many opinions was essentially destructive. There was no way he could follow a through line, and heaven knows what we did to his confidence.

The Joint Stock solution

Soon after this deflating experience, I became aware of a solution created by Max Stafford-Clark and William Gaskill with Joint Stock theatre company. They had evolved a unique process for developing new work with a writer. They began the project with a topic or theme, followed by a three-week exploration workshop with the writer present. Next the writer went off for several months to write a play on that theme but without obligation to use any material from the workshop. Naturally we can assume that the workshop would somehow have its influence, but essentially the writer was free to write the play they wanted to write. When the play was presented to the workshop actors, they could choose whether or not to continue in the production. Some stayed on, others declined. The results were often excellent. This was a fruitful process for many writers, including Caryl Churchill, who wrote *Cloud Nine* and other plays through that process.

Adaptation

Anna Karenina

I am often asked to share my knowledge and experience of adapting novels. But my approach to adapting books for the stage has been largely confined to my work with writer Helen Edmundson.

When I first came to Shared Experience Theatre in 1989 as their new artistic director, Mike Alfreds, its founder, had been running the company for twelve years. I was aware of his brilliant track record in adapting novels such as *Bleak House* and *A Handful of Dust* for the stage. In fact, when the RSC had a major success in 1980 with their six-hour version of *Nicholas Nickleby*, many in the theatre community felt the production owed its invention and style of performance to Alfreds's work. It was exciting to see how fringe theatre was influencing the mainstream; however, I was not sure I would be following that route.

When watching a book adaptation, I was concerned that I was continually reminded that we were watching a book rather than a play. I wondered if this was uncomfortable for those in the audience who had never read it. Did they feel ignorant or at a disadvantage in relation to those who knew the book? My concern led me to a commitment to solely performing plays. But I soon became discouraged when we were failing to achieve touring dates. In our search for between six and eight theatres which would present us for week-long runs on the mid-scale circuit, we seemed increasingly unable to propose titles that venues found attractive or different enough from what other companies were offering. In frustration I came to a decision: 'Right, we will offer a famous book, let them turn that down!' And I was keen to explore the challenge of adapting a book in a way that would leave behind its narrative voice so that it became a fully fledged piece of drama.

My first thought was *Anna Karenina*. I had always adored Tolstoy's great novel, and I knew the Glasgow Citizens Theatre had produced it. I hoped to read and maybe acquire their version as a starting point, but soon discovered that they were not happy with it and it was no longer available for performance.

What a lucky moment that was for me, because it began a search for a new writer who could adapt Tolstoy's work. When I met Helen Edmundson I presented her with a challenge: 'Look at this adaptation as if you were doing a ballet or an opera of the book. Feel free to take huge liberties. Your only commitment is to be inspired by Tolstoy's *Anna Karenina*, but you have no obligation to revere it or serve it. In fact you should assume that you might be offending people who love this book. You may very well be accused of defilement.' I wanted to free the writer from serving the book so that she could create something completely theatrical.

Helen was the perfect choice for this venture. At no point did she use a narrator's voice. And she fittingly described what she was writing as a 'play' in its own right. To our delight, so many who loved the book were enthralled by what we had created. *Anna Karenina* was a major success for Shared Experience, which toured later to Australia, Malaysia, Prague, Buenos Aires and New York.

- In Chapter 7, I examine the process of adapting and designing *Anna Karenina*.

Subsequently Helen and I worked together on many adaptations: *Mill on the Floss*, *Gone to Earth*, *Orestes* and *War and Peace* (for the National Theatre). And we collaborated on an original play in 2012, *The Heresy of Love*. Previously, at the RSC, I had directed *House of Desires*, a comedy by the remarkable Sor Juana Inés de la Cruz, a seventeenth-century Mexican nun. Her extraordinary and challenging life intrigued me and I encouraged the RSC to commission Helen to write a play about her.

The Heresy of Love is a big, ambitious piece, stunning in its breadth, its wisdom, its humour, and it was a major success for the RSC. Perhaps there had been few hopes for its appeal and so sadly it had only seventeen performances in the Swan Theatre in the dead of winter. I fought long and hard for it to have a further life, to no avail. It is a great sadness, as I believe Helen's play to be a major piece of work by a woman writer – a rarity in our times. It needs a large company, but few theatres are in a position to take that on.

2

The concept

Defining what the play is about in one sentence is for me an essential starting point. I remember reading about the team that created the musical *Fiddler on the Roof* and how they struggled with choreographer Jerome Robbins's insistence that they dig deeper to discover what the musical was 'about'. They finally settled on the idea that it was essentially about tradition. And indeed the song *Tradition* became the opening number of the show.

I believe this attempt to define the piece is essentially a search for a concept which will guide choices and decision making. Synonyms for 'concept' might be 'view' or 'approach', perhaps described as a 'take' on the play. This need for a concept is particularly necessary when remounting a well-known classic which has been produced hundreds of times and may be very well known to audiences. When working with designers I have certainly found the need for a concept; I am keen for the set, sound and lighting to express what the play is about.

For example: *Half Life* by John Mighton, which I directed in 2016 for Theatre Royal Bath's Ustinov Studio, was set in a retirement home. Two of its main characters were slightly confused about time, reality and their personal history. When designer Janet Bird and I were working on the set, she introduced a physical image which expressed the characters' confusion. Whereas the bulk of the set was completely realistic, armchairs for seniors, similar to those on set, were suspended from the ceiling at different heights and angles. The effect was disorienting and helped to subtly express the characters' inner state.

When Polly Teale and I were co-directing *Mill on the Floss* for Shared Experience, our adapter Helen Edmundson requested a set with an upper level as she was starting the play with a community who were attempting to drown a woman to prove whether or not she was a witch. This image was central to the story as its main character, Maggie Tulliver, was intent on living life to the full at a time when any woman stepping out of line was in danger of being rejected by her community or indeed tried as a witch.

I remember with great pleasure the eureka moment of thinking: 'Let's make the set a place for testing a witch.' The upper level became a bridge perfect for that purpose. The floor became a painted cloth which resembled a river bed with half-sunken bits of furniture and household objects scattered on its surface. The bridge supports were clearly water-marked where they would be below the water level. The whole play took place in and around this river bed and its bridge. The set now expressed the concept – what the play was about.

A classic: Digging for the concept

How do I connect with a well-known classic in such a way that gives it meaning and relevance for today? I am not interested in a museum experience, a trip back in time. My goal is to engage with its timeless elements, the very aspects that make us want to revive it in the twenty-first century.

It might sound limiting to be choosing one single concept, but early on I learned the danger of wanting to make your production about everything in the play that excites or interests you. When I was directing Euripides' *The Bacchae*, my first production as artistic director of Shared Experience, I had the luxury of a long rehearsal period. The more I read about the play, the more detail I wanted to include in my production. But I had so many ideas about the play and its layers of meaning that I had no filter, no reason to reject anything. When my designer would suggest an element for the set, I had no guiding principle to help me assess that element and what it was saying or contributing. In fact, today my memory of the set makes me cringe with embarrassment; we were trying to include too many ideas. I now understand that so much freedom can be dizzying; it becomes hard to select or to define a specific aim with the piece. But if I had settled on a basic concept, choices would have fallen into place. Paradoxically, restrictions can be freeing.

So how do I discover or tease out a concept which will be a particular take on what the play wants, a concept which I can share with the actors to give them a sense of a common aim, a purpose, a need to perform this play? Inside the play there is something human and enlightening and if we in the company can share that, it will guide all aspects of the work. It will affect set design, casting, lighting, music, sound – virtually every element that makes up a production.

Needless to say, each director must find something essential in the play that suggests their particular concept. Finding a concept that works for you is a lonely business, but this is perhaps the one area that needs to be a personal choice. And, of course, a great play will be full of many possible choices. If by chance a director revisits a play ten years after their first production, more often than not they will connect with the play in a different way, demanding a fresh concept.

Case study

Finding the concept for *All's Well that Ends Well*

Shakespeare's plays are a particular challenge as they are many-layered and dense with possible themes to tease out. In 2013 I was invited to direct Shakespeare's *All's Well that Ends Well* for the Royal Shakespeare Company in its redesigned large auditorium. With *All's Well* often regarded as a problem play, partly because of its inconsistent story telling, it is no surprise that recent productions had been mounted in the small Swan Theatre. Perhaps it was not considered a 'popular' play for audiences. This was to be its first major outing in the large space since the great Peggy Ashcroft had played the Countess thirty-one years before.

Clearly the play presents a challenge. Events don't always connect or make sense. Character behaviour can be unreal or fantastical. The language is often convoluted and hard to decipher. Its privileged, wealthy hero, young Bertram, behaves badly and has very few redeeming features. He is adored by young Helena, who resorts to trickery in order to trap him into a relationship. Her obsessive love for Bertram can be unappealing to an audience. Although I was thrilled by the offer to direct this play, I confess to feeling apprehensive when I was asked to take it on.

Okay, I told myself. Read the play. Read it carefully, minutely. Try at the most basic level to understand what people are saying to each other. As I began reading painstakingly, little things began to jump out which surprised and intrigued me. The play was written around 1605. Young Bertram is obsessed with becoming a soldier and going off to war. I wondered about young noblemen at that time and their attitude to a soldier's life. In the play an adviser to the King of France is helping the king decide whether or not to take sides in another country's war. He explains to the king that young men have a crying need to assert themselves, so perhaps a war would be useful: 'It may well serve as a nursery to our gentry, who are sick for breathing and exploit.' The king sees sense in this advice. Young noblemen are languishing in their desperate need to discover themselves through action. Today we can easily relate to this situation: young men, 16–21-year-olds full of testosterone, needing to flex certain muscles, muscles for dominance. Sport can play its part in their lives, but so can warlike activities, evidenced by gang culture and football hooliganism. These are timeless explosive drives.

As I found more evidence for this thread, I questioned the usual response to young Bertram's character. Because he refuses Helena's love in a way that can seem snobbish, rude and uncaring, because he goes to huge lengths to seduce a another young woman who is resisting him, because he lies his way out of sticky situations, Bertram is usually written off as unattractive and unappealing. But I began to find hints in the text which encouraged me to see him differently.

When we meet Bertram he is stricken by the recent death of his father. He is a very young man with a huge desire to prove himself, keen to sow wild oats. He is running a mile from the idea of marriage, and needs desperately to define himself, to be a soldier, to go to war.

Bertram in *All's Well that Ends Well*

Act 2, Scene 1 – Bertram complains he is too young to join the soldiers:
I am commanded here, and kept a coil with 'Too young' and 'the next year' and 'tis too early.'

Act 2, Scene 5 – Bertram runs away to war. To Helena:
Go thou towards home
Where I shall never come
Whilst I can shake my sword
Or hear the drum.

Act 3, Scene 3 – Bertram's pledge to the god of war:
This very day,
Great Mars I put myself into thy file;
Make me but like my thoughts and I shall prove
A lover of thy drum, a hater of love.

Although Bertram is often seen as selfish and deceitful and uncaring, I now found myself judging him less harshly. This discovery, a bit of gold, was opening doors. I was discovering my personal 'take' on *All's Well that Ends Well*.

Months later I was gratified to learn that I had taken some of the audience with me in my thinking about Bertram. At a post-show discussion, a woman in the audience expressed her disapproval of this young man. Frankly, I was disappointed that my concept of Bertram had not landed. So I asked if everyone in the audience agree with her and to my delight two women seated together at the back of the stalls raised their hands. 'No,' one of them said, 'we have sons.' How brilliant that they were reminded of their young sons, exploring life wildly and passionately. It seems they recognized Bertram's bad behaviour, but they also saw his youth, his humanity, his needs.

When the eminent Shakespeare scholar and author James Shapiro came to our rehearsals at the RSC, he corroborated this take on Bertram. Shapiro's books on Shakespeare, in particular *1599*, have been hugely inspirational to so many and I felt privileged to have him present the company with an introduction to *All's Well that Ends Well*. I was particularly grateful that we were able to have a pre-chat. Shapiro wanted to hear my approach to the play, to make sure he would not be contradicting me or confusing the company.

We learned that in Shakespeare's day most young gentlemen would actively pursue a chance to prove themselves by going to war. Also, Bertram's wholesale rejection of marriage made sense, as men in Elizabethan times rarely married before their late twenties. Perhaps we understand Bertram's horror of early marriage even better when we note that Shakespeare was married at the age of 18 to a woman who was ten years older and pregnant with his child.

At the time I was grateful for James Shapiro's thoughtfulness, especially coming from someone bringing such a huge store of historical knowledge. He made every effort to understand my 'take' on the play. And it taught me in future the need to collaborate with experts before they speak to the company. I have to add that there is always a danger when an expert comes to give a talk about historical background that they may not be interested in hearing your concept or ideas. And they might have very fixed attitudes about the play. So it is worth being on guard and making an attempt to talk things through beforehand. In the most extreme cases I have found the experience disruptive and had to speak to the company after the 'talk' and explain my different perspective.

Women's perspective

How about the women in the play, what would that yield in my search for a concept? Unsurprisingly the women were not interested in a soldier's life, but Bertram's widowed mother, the Countess, is extremely selfless and nurturing. She has a great capacity for love. Helena, her young and penniless ward, is obsessed and in love with Bertram. I have since learned that there is no other woman in Shakespeare who so actively pursues the person they love. (Even Helena in *A Midsummer Night's Dream* is pursuing someone who had previously wooed her.) I began to see Helena and the Countess as characters driven by love, and then noticed how the smaller female characters were bonding together and looking after each other in a loving way. So a concept was taking shape. Male energy obsessed with dominance, making one's mark, i.e. war. Female energy obsessed with nurturing and giving, i.e. love.

Fairy-tale mode

How about the fairy-tale elements in the play, the bits of magic and unexplained connections, Helena using a bed-trick to trick Bertram into sleeping with her? Could they be part of the overall concept? Could this be put into one sentence? Perhaps: 'A fairy tale of love and war.' That might seem simple, but it included all the war and love imagery plus the fairy-tale style of storytelling. The marketing department at the RSC later developed this idea and created a blurb: *A Beguiling Fairy Tale of Love and War*.

Once the concept emerges, one can feel more confident about starting work with a designer. Without a concept, those meetings can feel unfocused, but if I can bring a concept to the table, it becomes my guiding principle. In this case the concept was to stage a fairy tale in which *love* as female energy and *war* as male energy are huge forces which collide and intersect.

Shakespeare – the cut

Once I had ploughed through *All's Well*, I was able to research previous RSC production scripts to see how other directors had edited this confused, knotty play. It was a great help, studying their choices. In fact the task of doing your own edit of a Shakespeare work is an especially organic way to experience the play. I felt like a detective, examining previous director cuts, thinking about them, evaluating them, and finally making my own decisions. Previous cuts are often available by getting in touch with individual theatres where the play has recently been produced.

In 2017 the highly original and sometimes controversial director Emma Rice was running Shakespeare's Globe when she invited me to direct *King Lear*. To my surprise I was offered a unique choice: a significant sum added onto my directing fee for my dramaturgical work and cutting of the play, or the same sum to be given to a freelance dramaturg. I grabbed this opportunity. I knew Patrick Sandford, former artistic director of the Nuffield Theatre Southampton, as a hugely experienced director and writer. His research, support and assistance in cutting this great play made an enormous contribution to the project.

Casting

There is a well-worn adage in the theatre world which claims that casting accounts for 80 per cent of your success in mounting a play. I certainly agree that it is hugely important and when you get it wrong, achieving your hopes for the piece can be a losing battle.

Whenever possible I would choose to have someone working alongside me when casting. For many years – far too long – I ran casting sessions on my own, but eventually learned the value of sharing the process. It is a great help to have someone who can read the script aloud opposite the actor, which leaves one free to observe. My favoured process now is to meet the actor for a short meeting, say ten minutes, looking at a scene or two. Ideally the actor will have been told which scenes to look at. Next, I would test out how flexible and open they were by asking them to read again with a different approach: more angry, less aware, more ambivalent, etc. Afterwards, if my helper is my producer or if the writer is present, I can discuss the audition with them, and then have call-backs another day for the few actors who stand out by the end of the session.

Recent developments in the industry have now introduced a process whereby actors send in self-tapes and are then invited to an in-person session for call-backs. It is hard to think this can be totally satisfying.

Casting directors

When I have the luxury of a casting director, I first discuss how I see each character, which helps them to make their lists of actors for me to meet. Later, we discuss the auditions. As the casting director gradually gains a sense of what qualities I am looking for, this can be a fruitful learning process for us both. If I know this casting director's work, having seen other shows they have cast, I will have formed an opinion about their values and taste in actors. However, if I am working at a theatre which assigns me a casting director, it will take time to discover their taste and preferences.

Some directors are able to do a full day of auditions, with actors coming in every ten minutes. Although I have tried to work that way, I now know I cannot function well under that kind of pressure. I would prefer a session to last a few hours and would invite actors every twenty minutes, giving time for reflection and chat before moving on to the next.

Beware a situation where a forceful casting director works hard to influence your choices. Casting is a delicate process, and someone else's opinion can sway you from your best instincts. Naturally directors are grateful when they can work again and again with the same casting directors. Trust and understanding grows.

Casting mistakes

At any time in rehearsal I can be distracted by the thought that I have made a big mistake in casting. There so many elements at play when this happens. If things are not working well, if an actor seems unable to grasp the character, if they seem lacking in a quality essential to the role, it can feel like a losing battle just getting from A to B. If I think that I chose this particular actor because of forceful urging from the casting director, I will feel particularly stressed that I had not followed my own judgement.

However, if I had been very keen to cast the actor and highly impressed with their audition, I will want to honour my first impression and work hard to bring them to a level of performance I had imagined when we first met. It is a lot easier to live with your mistakes when they are your own. What is difficult is living with your mistakes when you have failed to trust your instincts.

Indeed, casting is such a subjective, mysterious process, it is no wonder the rehearsal is endlessly surprising. When you are working with actors new to you, so many things can unfold. A slow starter can grow organically into a full rich performance. A bold starter can lose confidence mid-rehearsal and need psychological support to get them through to a better place. An actor can be resistant at first, but gradually come to trust you and the process. It is always a pleasure to work with an actor a second time, when you have learnt their process and they are full of confidence knowing that you have chosen to work with them again.

3

Keystones: Ensemble, wants, obstacles and status

On the first day of rehearsal a crowd comes together in the rehearsal room. They are working for the theatre or for the production company and they have been invited for the 'meet and greet', to be introduced and to meet the cast. The designer will present and explain the set; costume drawings may be shown. Given that most of us are strangers to each other, this first day can be stressful and disorienting. With nerves running so high, I wonder how much the actors are able to take in. Many of them are in a state of terror, or at the very least high tension, anticipating the read-through that is about to happen. There are many things to be anxious about: perhaps having to read in an unfamiliar accent; uncertainty as to how much a performance is expected for that first reading; exposing oneself to a roomful of strangers.

In regard to actors feeling uneasy, I need to remind myself that their lives can be full of rejection. Worse than actual rejection, they often audition and never hear back either a 'yes' or a 'no' – a demoralizing experience which they have to survive over and over again. Added to this, every time they work with a new director they are being asked to trust and to follow someone they do not know, whose method of work is new to them. In addition we want them to open themselves emotionally, to bare their souls in the rehearsal room and finally to the public. Regardless of the confident or arrogant front they might present in a rehearsal room, I need to remember their vulnerability.

As the read-through is a tense experience at the best of times and I, the director, am also in a state of nervous excitement, often it feels best to just get through it as cheerfully as possible. Nowadays many directors do the 'meet and greet' but save the reading for the second day. I prefer to read on the first day and let all those who are working on the production hear the piece read aloud. I also prefer to get the nerves of the reading over with as soon as possible. But on day two, when I am on my own with the company, we can begin proper rehearsal. We can start to build an ensemble.

Why ensemble?

I believe an audience is most deeply engaged in a performance when the actors are palpably working together. Ensemble can be a general term and may have a vague meaning for people. In sharing my concept of ensemble and introducing my ethos to the company, I focus first on the word 'play'. We theatre people use the word 'play' to describe a piece of work, and we also talk about 'playing' a role. However in daily life 'play' is used differently; it describes interacting with others in an extremely pleasurable way, playfully.

Children play together with huge energy, often creating alternative worlds and situations. When athletes in a football match concentrate on playing together rather than as individuals, they achieve more. Doubles partners in tennis need to play together in order to win; nowadays doubles partners will often touch hands after every point in order to physically remind themselves that they are supporting each other and that even when a point has just been lost, they are playing together as a team. I explain to the actors that we in the theatre need to achieve a similar quality of play to that which we see in sport – teams bringing exciting energy to the work by bouncing off each other. As we find this sort of interaction thrilling when we play games or observe sport, can we achieve this same excitement when we play together as actors so that we engage the audience deeply? How can we transport them and take them with us on our journey?

I often give the example of an audience chatting together when leaving a performance and commenting about what they have seen. We might hear someone say 'I liked the boy', or 'The mother was good'. Alternatively, if the piece has been performed by an ensemble who are honestly working off each other, the comments might be more about the whole experience and its impact. At least this is something we can hope for. That is the aim.

During rehearsal I want to inspire a company to commit to the production as a whole. I share my ideas about the play with them, my personal take on it. When the set designer shows them the set, I explain to the company how the set expresses these ideas. If we all have a sense of what the play is wanting to say and what this production hopes to convey, we can work together to give the audience a very special experience. It just might free a few actors from thinking that this particular job is primarily about their career or a stepping stone to other work. I give myself a goal: to inspire the company towards a common purpose. As we work, my hope is that we will come together in the true meaning of ensemble.

Of course, building an ensemble and a sense of common purpose takes time and I must allow for that. If there are disruptive elements in the room or if an actor does not trust me as director, building a sense of common purpose can seem like a very tall order. Whatever the success rate, I do believe it is worth the effort.

Exercises

There are many exercises for creating ensemble.

Whenever possible in the first day or two, any game which requires people to make eye contact is great as an ice-breaker.

I am a firm believer in the value of eye contact. In new situations, many people avoid it out of shyness.

- Life stories: The company sits in a circle. All at the same time and in pairs one person tells the other person their life story in one minute, timed by me. Then we go around the circle and I ask the receiving person in each pair to tell the group what they can remember of their partner's life story. Repeat the exercise with change of roles. Hopefully this opens the company to further conversations during breaks. If there is an odd number in the group, I pair with the extra person.

- Telling lies: The company sits in a circle. I ask one person to choose another, look straight at them and tell them three things about themselves, one of which is a lie – e.g. 'I was born in Manchester'; 'My mother was a champion figure skater'; 'I have two cats'. The person receiving the information tries to guess which is the lie. If they get it wrong, ask if someone else wants to guess the lie. This can be very amusing. Next the receiving person chooses someone in the circle and tells them three things about themselves, one being a lie, etc. This game is enjoyable and it means people are using eye contact and really seeing each other. Eventually I point out that people often do some odd physical tic when they are lying (a well-known phenomenon in poker games), which makes everyone extra observant.

- Physical awareness: Simple physical games for a group that will relax everyone; ball-throwing games; walking about the space and trying to sense each other so that you all stop at the same time. A pause, then without words make a collective decision to resume walking. Repeat several times.

- Seeing each other: Stand opposite someone who is telling you a story and try to imitate their words, speaking along with them immediately and exactly. I suggest the 'story' could be a favourite film or 'what I had for breakfast and how I travelled to rehearsal'. I encourage the follower to take on all physical gesture as well. After a few minutes, change roles. Then make new pairings to do the same exercise. When people misunderstand this exercise they speak very slowly, so I move around to each group encouraging the speaker to talk at a fairly normal pace and I encourage the follower to copy all physical gesture. This game encourages people to really see and hear each other.

- Paper charades: Create small groups of 4 or 5 and have them play paper charades. Ask each group to write on paper several charades for another group, for example *The Sound of Music*. Fold up the written charades and hand them to another group. One person opens a charade. That person may not speak. They draw on paper as the others watch and try to guess out loud the title. The sketcher can draw a symbol for film, theatre, book. They can mark out the number of words. The others in their group may speak as they prompt the drawer to try more sketches to help them guess the answer. When I have a wide variety of ages in the room I have often used paper charades as an ice-breaker and to relax people. Older actors might find physical games too uncomfortable but this one feels safe and fun.

- In Chapter 4, I give examples of the following types of improvisation:
  - Short improvisations where each character is put into a modern-day situation and the actor can thus explore character *wants*.
  - Full company improvisation on a moment in time for the characters in the play.

Difficulty of ensemble work in big companies

How exciting to work for a company like the RSC where you are directing a big play in a large theatre with a company of twenty-three actors. It is thrilling to have all the resources you could possibly want. Rehearsals might be as long as eight to ten weeks. The backup from technical staff is remarkable, rehearsal props appear almost as soon as they are thought of. The designer can create from scratch entire new worlds of costume or furniture design. The composer will attend rehearsal on a regular basis. You will have the luxury of a three- or four-person stage management team backing up rehearsals. The small part actors are all understudying main roles. All of this is truly luxurious if most of your working life as a director has provided only a tiny fraction of these elements.

So what are the challenges? To be sure, many of them will come as a surprise.

Creating an ensemble can be totally idealistic, creative and possible in low-budget rehearsal situations. One of the great joys is sharing your working ethos with a group of people and bringing them to a point where they are all working with similar aims and understanding. But it is almost impossible to create an ensemble with a group of actors who have been hired for a season of plays and are already in performance. If an RSC season has between six and eight plays and your actors are in some of those plays, their energies and concentration are fractured. If they come to your rehearsal each morning having performed a long play the night before, they will be tired. And during your rehearsal they are by necessity saving some of their energy for the upcoming performance that night. In the best scenario, everyone is positive and works hard, but a long season where a company is performing eight shows a week will always be particularly draining.

I remember too well one boiling hot afternoon, rehearsing a full company scene at the RSC in the beautiful wood-beamed

Ashcroft Room with its windows overlooking the river Avon. While I was taking a few minutes to work out a moment between two characters, several of the waiting actors lay down mid-floor to rest until they were needed. This might have felt disrespectful, but it was an extremely hot day and I was mindful that they were thoroughly exhausted. In fact I was glad they felt so comfortable in my rehearsal room that they could do such a thing.

My solution to their arduous schedule and depleted energy levels was to schedule the first rehearsals of the day with actors who had not been performing the night before. And I looked forward hugely to the period when we finally moved into technical rehearsals and previews. Only then could my actors concentrate exclusively on the piece we were working on and begin to function as an ensemble.

Wants, obstacles, status

In the first days of rehearsal I introduce several keystones. These main tools which I share with the company are the building blocks that give a sound base to the work. Given that rehearsal periods can be quite short, exercises serve well to introduce these approaches: the Wants, Obstacles, and Status exercises.

Wants

When we human beings are closely observed, it makes us self-conscious. We lose our ability to be natural, to be totally ourselves. This self-consciousness makes playing a part before an audience quite a challenge. The more you can believe you are actually another person, the more free you might feel. But the most powerful way to lose self-consciousness is to find a task, something you are trying to achieve, to make happen.

This was made dramatically clear to me during an exercise I experienced in a valuable acting workshop led by Julia Bardsley. I hasten to add that although I would use this exercise with students, I would rarely use it in rehearsal as it is basically a training exercise for actors who are just starting out. In a professional company this exercise might feel overly simplistic.

Half of us were asked to form a line in front of the other half of the class, who were seated observing us closely, studying us. We felt exposed, self-conscious; we didn't know how to present ourselves to these watchers. Trying to relax and seem normal was exceedingly uncomfortable and a bit embarrassing.

Next the leader gave us a task: look closely at the watchers and see if any of them have tiny tics or habits you can pick up on. Choose one, begin to do it back to the watching group, and as you slowly back away (several metres) from the watchers make it bigger, exagerate it. Then as you slowly return across the floor to your original position, allow the tic to reduce gradually, becoming smaller and smaller. Because we had a specific task, we had become totally engaged and had lost our self-consciousness. This was so simple, but it was a revelation.

In this exercise we were operating as ourselves, but as actors we would have to go further to operate as a character. And it would be a next step to give that character a task to achieve. Here was a way to experience the power of having an objective. I describe this exercise here because it illustrates the concept of having a task, an aim.

When I am working professionally, most actors would hopefully have learned either through training or experience what it means to play an objective/desire/target etc. So I start by acknowledging that the language and exercises I use might feel like old ground, but as we are a new group we may have very different ideas of what this terminology means to each person. I take the time to share my understanding of what it means to play a task or objective (later to be called the 'want'). This is the main starting point that underpins all the work.

Stanislavski

'Super-objective' and 'objective' are two potent terms which have come down to us from Konstantin Stanislavski, the great Russian actor/director and creator of what we call method acting. His basics are still the bedrock teaching on many drama courses. Over the years I have encountered alternatives to his words, some more user-friendly than others. His use of the word 'objective' for the big overall life want of the character can sound intellectual, dry, lacking in feeling. In fact I recently learned that the word Stanislavski used in Russian was *zadacha*, which translates as task or goal, but somehow in English translation it had become 'objective'. Whatever its origins, the objective when used properly can be a powerful tool to access and release emotion. Here are some words often used for objective: intention; action; desire; target; need – and there are probably many others.

In the 1990s my directing colleague Polly Teale was using another word for the super-objective: the *big want* – this is an overall life want; and for the objective: the *want* – this is the *want* for each scene. I found this attractive. By renaming the objective and calling it a *want*, those who might have had little or no training could connect more easily with the question 'What does your character *want*?' than they could with 'What is your character's objective or intention?' And those who had their own training and their own vocabulary were not threatened when I used the word '*want*'. In time I began referring to the super-objective and scene objective as the *big want* and the *want*.

For me, these wants are crucial. Without this foundation, the work can become sprawling and discursive. But with them, I can lead the rehearsal and focus the work from moment to moment. I will later talk about obstacles, as it is the tension between your want and the obstacles to your want that creates dramatic tension.

Wants: Conscious and subconscious

In her excellent book *Respect for Acting*, Uta Hagen, the great actor and teacher, introduces the idea of the conscious objective and the subconscious objective. I recommend her book to every class or company I work with. I shall now refer, as she does, to the conscious want and the subconscious want. When we look for the subconscious want, we are searching for what the character does not know about themselves. Hitler, for example, may have said aloud to others that he wanted to make Germany into a great leader of nations, but we might say that subconsciously he wanted power, to dominate.

I find it essential early on to settle on the wants with the actors. In the first days of rehearsal we sit in a circle and talk ideas through until we are in agreement. Ideally I would try to make these choices in an extended discussion, starting with the actor who is playing the role and then encouraging others to join in. In a play with many characters, I would lead early discussions about the big want with everyone present and participating, but then move on to discussing character wants in smaller groups, often as a first step to looking at a scene, and always with the proviso that one can change one's mind about that chosen want as rehearsals progress.

Defining the big want

The big want (Stanislavski's overall super-objective) is what the character desires most in life, a goal they would sacrifice anything to achieve. It is defined by how they would like to be perceived in their milieu and in the world. In order to find the big want, I encourage actors to ponder what their character want would have been around the age of 20, possibly way before the play begins. If we look at Shakespeare's Hamlet at that age, we can think about what his big life want was as he entered manhood. At that young age, who was Hamlet? What did he *want* from life? What mattered to him more than anything? This will help us define his *big want* when we come to the play, when his circumstances have become demanding and extreme.

Hamlet's want at 20

Prince Hamlet is a complex character, inspiring a dazzling range of interpretations. We can posit many possible choices of

want for this character. In the play we meet Hamlet at a point
of crisis, when he is struggling with great obstacles and trials,
and it would be tempting to see his big want coming from the
crisis he is dealing with, but here are possibilities for Hamlet at
age 20.

Conscious: *I want to be true to myself*
Subconscious: *Wants his father's respect*

Conscious: *I want to become a great leader of my country*
Subconscious: *Wants to be respected and admired*

Conscious: *I want my father to be proud of me*
Subconscious: *Wants love*

Hamlet when we meet him

When we meet Prince Hamlet at the start of Shakespeare's
play, his father has died suddenly and his uncle Claudius
has taken over the kingdom. Within weeks of Hamlet's
father dying, his mother has married this same uncle. The
ghost of Hamlet's father has appeared in the night, revealing
that he had been murdered and begging Hamlet to avenge his
death.

As I mentioned, the temptation would be to define Hamlet's
big want (remember this is a life want) in terms of his present
situation.

Conscious: *I want to avenge my father's death*
Subconscious: *Wants love*

But I believe that this choice falls into the trap of being defined
by the plot of the play, rather than a want that Hamlet had as
a person long before his father had been murdered. I would
encourage the actor to return to the wants we had posited for
him above, when he was 20 years old, to see if they gave a
bigger sense of what drives him as a person.

How the want accesses emotion

Why are wants the base for all the work? When an actor is playing a role and desiring to feel something – love, anger, jealousy, doubt, etc. – concentrating on the want will bring forth the emotion. This is a challenging concept for student actors to take on, as their first idea might be to 'act' as though they are feeling the emotion. Act sad. Act happy. Act frightened. Act angry. But Stanislavski's concept of the objective or intention (which I am calling the want) is the most truthful route into accessing emotion – emotion that you feel honestly and in the body.

In life when we are sad or angry it is unlikely that we would say we 'want' to have those feelings. When we cry, often we are trying to stop crying. If an actor is working hard to shed tears in a role and is pleased when they come, it is unlikely that the emotion will touch us or seem true. Given that a strong want is the route to accessing emotions, perhaps the actor needs to get in touch with a deeper want, one more connected to emotion they have experienced in their lives.

Want questions:
What do I want?
Why do I want it?
How will I get it?

If in life I am attempting to rescue a friend who is destroying their life with alcohol and I am trying to get them to join Alcoholics Anonymous, what is my want? The actor might choose to play things like: 'I am sensible. I am caring. I am upset with you.' Those choices are what I refer to as 'description': the actor is merely describing behaviour. But these choices are not wants. If the actor is working with a strong want and raising the stakes, their want could be: 'I want to save you from destroying yourself.' Playing such a strong want will in most cases access true emotion, particularly if the actor can go to the make-believe place all actors need where they remember life experiences or imagine talking to a dear friend or relative while fearing for their safety.

Changing the want

Beware the actor who has changed their mind about their want, without sharing with you, the director. When this has happened, it becomes apparent in rehearsal. I need to emphasize how important it is to re-examine the choice and come to agreement on the want. As a director, I find much of my time in the early days is spent reminding the actor of their want and urging them to give it primary focus.

In Martin Sherman's excellent adaptation of *A Passage to India*, Penny Layden was playing Adela Quested. I knew Penny to be an extremely accomplished actor who would only feel comfortable when she knew her want and was playing it to the full. We both felt there was one scene that was not working. There was no tension. It felt like the character was disappearing. Penny and I discussed the problem and after some trial and error came to agree that Adela needed a different want in that scene. These sorts of discussions are fruitful when they lead to a deeper investigation of character, a more three-dimensional insight into how human beings cope with life-changing experiences.

For early exploration of the character want, improvisation can be a great help. But it is not always possible, particularly if there are actors in the room who have a real antipathy to improvisation.

- I deal with improvisation as a tool in Chapter 5.

Seeing the want: The chair exercise

As I approach rehearsal, I then move on to discuss the character's want for the whole play. It will be closely linked to the big want and followed up by the want for each scene. The want for each scene is a step on the way for the character to achieve their life or play want.

In my desire to illustrate the importance of playing the objective/want I often use an exercise I call the 'chair exercise'. This exercise is performed in pairs without words.

The two actors, Al and Bea, sit in identical simple chairs next to each other facing the audience. I point out that there is little story we can divine from observing them. However when I shift the position of a chair so that Al is now facing Bea at a slight distance, we see a story emerging. 'If this were a painting,' I ask, 'what story are we telling or perceiving?' Perhaps Al wants something from Bea. Perhaps Bea is refusing Al. I point out that we each might see different stories, but the change in position is creating the story. Now we are communicating without words, through chair position. If I want to play a want, to affect you, I need to place my chair in a position that might help me achieve my goal.

I take the exercise further by giving each actor a strong want. The situation: Al and Bea are a couple. Bea has been flirting with Al's's best friend. Al is angry. Their wants?

Al *wants* to punish Bea
Bea *wants* to be forgiven.

Al places his chair and sits on it in a position that says: 'I want to punish.'
Bea enters and places her chair in a position that says: 'I want your forgiveness.' Bea sits.

Al answers with a new position and sits.
Bea answers with a new position, etc.

As the answering continues this becomes a conversation, each person trying to achieve their want or goal. As the two wants are in strong opposition, conflict intensifies.

I often have to prompt during the exercise. I will pause it and ask the actors and then the watchers how strongly on a scale of 1–100 per cent do they think the actor is playing their want. Often the want is quite weak and I encourage them to play the want 100 per cent.

Once a few pairs have tried this exercise, with other scenarios, I will add in *obstacles,* explained in the next section.

Al *wants* to punish, but his *obstacle* is a fear that he will lose Bea.
Bea *wants* forgiveness, but her *obstacle* is that she is irritated with Al.

It works well to have more pairs trying this same situation, changing the sexes and also having them the same sex. Introducing this exercise early in rehearsals, I can feel confident that I have emphasized the importance of having the *wants* and *obstacles* as building blocks for the work. And, significantly, this is an exercise where we can actually see the wants and obstacles rather than discuss them.

Love or power?

A fine and inspiring teacher/director, Mladen Materic, once posited that the big want is always about one of two things: love or power. This is thought-provoking and often true. Here are some examples of character big wants including the conscious and subconscious. Keep in mind that these are simply possibilities.

Macbeth
Conscious: *I want to be admired and respected forever as a great king of Scotland*
Subconscious: *Wants power*

Titania in *A Midsummer Night's Dream*
Conscious: *I want to regain my freedom in my woodland fairy world*
Subconscious: *Wants power*

Willy Loman in *Death of a Salesman*
Conscious: *I want to be respected/to win*
Subconscious: *Wants to be loved and admired*

Martha (age 20) in *Who's Afraid of Virginia Woolf?*
Conscious: *I want complete charge of my life*
Subconscious: *Wants freedom and power*

Natasha in War and Peace

So often actors come to rehearsal and are keen to share everything they have been thinking and researching on their own – a mountain of ideas. Of course I am pleased that they are investigating, not waiting for me to tell them what to do, but my first task is to lead them to a starting point. I listen to what they are offering and then bring it back to 'Okay, but what is the big want?' and 'What is your scene want?' Experienced, skilful actors can usually answer this. And it is always exciting for me when they suggest something original and unexpected.

In Helen Edmundson's adaptation for Shared Experience of Tolstoy's *War and Peace*, young Natasha is 13. She is passionate, full of mischief, playful, caring of others. She lights up a room with her radiant, mercurial energy, which can range from joy to despair in an instant. The actor needed to find a big want which would encompass these qualities. However there is a danger here. Being told that your character is charming and playful can be a burden. You might strive to enact those things, to play 'qualities'. But if you go down that route you will be describing your character rather than experiencing what motivates and drives her. When actors play qualities rather than wants, the work does not engage us or them. By qualities I mean things such as: I am charming. I am studious. I am sinister. I am sexy. I am unconfident. I am dangerous. These are qualities, but they are not active. They become mere description.

In our first production of *War and Peace*, young Anne-Marie Duff was playing Natasha. When challenged, she thought hard about her want and one day came in with a proposal: 'to challenge life'. It was an excellent choice which motivated Natasha in her ability to fill any room with activity and interaction, and included her generous need to look after everyone, her appetite for practical jokes, etc. With this strong big want, the actor will have purpose and tasks. She is freed from the chore of having to play qualities such as 'charming, funny, playful, dramatic'. Once the drive that motivates the big want is chosen, the work can begin.

The actor is lost

What about actors who cannot answer my question 'What is the want?' There are many who are at a loss to pinpoint this essential element. To them my request feels reductionist and mini, but I persist, as I believe we can only go forward by defining the wants. And of course we need to be in agreement about the choice.

In the early days of rehearsals, most actors are keen to be amenable. They will have a stab at coming up with wants, but if I find their suggestions lacking in drive, they will fairly happily go along with my suggestions. When possible I would follow this up with an exercise/improvisation where they would be able to experience this want on the floor. If they experience it, they might understand it in the deepest sense. Talking about a want is fine, but I suspect we don't always understand each other with words. If the actor can improvise the want, play it, act on it, there can be real comprehension.

Later in rehearsal if I feel an actor is unfocused or vague, I ask them to repeat their want. Very often they are at a loss and, as I suspected, have forgotten what we agreed in those early days. This is an indication that they are not really working with the want as their foundation and using it in a major way. I re-emphasize its importance.

Improvisation as a route to the want

Ross in *Macbeth* is a difficult character when it comes to defining his want. He acts as a trusted messenger, appearing often as a bringer of important news. He cares deeply about

Scotland. He starts out with respect and admiration for Macbeth. But when Macbeth becomes king and grows into a monster destroying his own country, Ross becomes distressed.

I was working with Liam, an actor who varied so enormously in what he offered in rehearsal that I came to believe he lacked a true sense of a want and what it meant to play it. For this character, Ross, I needed to help Liam and propose a strong want. I started out with: 'I *want* to be my country's guardian.' A subconscious want might be a desire for respect and love.

It became apparent that Liam was unable to take this suggested want and feel it as a driving force to take him through each scene. For him it was an idea only. In such cases I will often use improvisation in order to give the actor an experience of what it means to play a want powerfully as if their life depended on it. In Chapter 4 I describe the improvisation I used to help Liam access real drive as the character Ross.

Learning from the actor

When I was directing *A Comedy of Errors* for the RSC, I posited to the actors playing twin servants that their big want was to have power, to be freed from being a servant. As I had experienced when directing plays by Molière, there is much comedy to be mined in a servant's desire to dominate his master, especially when it leads to cheeky behaviour. To my surprise, one of the *Comedy of Errors* actors, Jonathan Slinger, contradicted me. He thought his character was different from his twin in that he was happy to be a servant and was keen to please his master, not dominate him. I confess that I was startled and could not assess this idea on the spot. But here was an experienced actor with a great comic sense, who had auditioned brilliantly for the role, so I was happy to go along with his idea and see where it led. In fact, it was an original and insightful approach, completely supported by the text. It was a clue to why Jonathan's very funny audition had stood out from so many others. A strong subconscious want for this servant clown might be 'to be loved and cherished'.

Obstacles

We have looked at the concept and practice of playing the want. And in life we can recognize that there are often obstacles to getting what we want, what we desire. 'I *want* this, but what will I need to overcome in order to get it?' If there are no obstacles to what we want, no resistance, there is no drama. Conflict is necessary for drama. It sometimes happens that an actor cannot grasp this or realize how important it is to have obstacles in a scene, either internally or from without.

If I want a luxurious rich lifestyle and I already have lots of money there is no obstacle, but this does not make for an interesting story. The story becomes dramatic when I have to overcome obstacles. How will I get the money? Beg a loan from a friend? Steal it? Charm someone? Cheat? Romeo and Juliet are in love. It is the obstacles to their love that engages us in their story, the danger to their lives if they dare to be together. The more pressure brought to bear on the protagonist, the more their actions reveal their character.

Obstacles can also be inner and outer, whatever prevents me from getting what I want. To mention a few sources: obstacles can come from previous circumstances (I was poor and am now lacking in confidence in high society); relationship (my partner dominates me and I can't confront him); weather (it is so hot I can barely function); time (I need to pack and leave quickly before someone arrives); health (I have breathing difficulties due to illness).

Stanley Kowalski: Wants and obstacles

Stanley Kowalski in Tennessee Williams's play *A Streetcar Named Desire* comes from a poor immigrant Polish background. We might see his character this way:

Big want
Conscious: *I want to be respected, to be king in my own home*
Subconscious: *Wants power, to dominate*

Obstacles
The world looks down on me, the 'dumb Polack'
Blanche sees me as common
I fear I will lose the love of Stella, my wife

Play the obstacle first

When an actor is working on a part, they can deepen the work by exploring the obstacles first. Later when they return to playing their objective (want) they will find they need to intensify their want in order to overcome those obstacles. This is a valuable exercise and I use it often in rehearsal.

An example: in Shakespeare's *Othello*, Lucy was playing Othello's young, honest wife Desdemona. Othello has come to distrust Desdemona, and she has become frightened of his rage. In the scene we were rehearsing, Desdemona is alone preparing for bed with her older companion Emilia. We started with this want: 'Even though I am afraid of Othello's rage and fear that I am losing his love, I want to be hopeful.' I felt it would be helpful if Lucy could explore the obstacle (her fear of losing Othello) first, so I asked her to forget her want for the moment and fully play her fear.

We read the scene again with Lucy concentrating on exploring her fear. Similarly I suggested an obstacle for her scene partner to play. This would feel strange because it is limiting the scene, but I explained to them that it was merely an exercise, that the scene would not work while they were reading it in this way. It was an exercise which would allow Lucy to experience the fear, the hidden underneath. Without this step we would have to ask the actor to think hard about the underneath and imagine its power; we would be asking her to do a lot of mental, thinking work. By contrast, this exercise allowed her to explore the obstacle (fear) and experience it – to sense it internally, in the body.

Next we went back to Lucy playing her want: to be positive and hopeful. Because she had played the obstacle first, she was still able to feel the fear physically bubbling inside her, bursting to get out. She now had to push this fear under and try to behave in a hopeful manner. As this was hard for Desdemona to achieve, the work became rich and layered. I should mention that I was able to work in this way because Lucy understood wants and was able to play them. If I were working with an actor whose want was weak, I would probably have to spend time on helping them to grasp the idea of the want. Adding obstacles too early would only be confusing.

Status

Here are the steps I use in order to share an idea of status and how to use it.

First, I explain status as it affects our daily lives. In any organization such as a school, a hospital, a business, there is usually an understood hierarchy from 1 to 10: 10 is high, 1 is low. In these hierarchies a lower number is expected to defer to a higher number. So in a school, the head teacher is a 10, the deputy head is a 9. As the teachers must defer to higher numbers, they are 7s and 8s. The older students (6, 5) are lower than these teachers. The younger students (4, 3) are even lower status and are expected to defer to older students, teachers, etc.

To get people thinking, I always ask the group what number the school caretaker would be. The initial response might be a 6 or 7, but we know that any organization is going to be majorly dependent on the person who looks after cleanliness and their personal safety. So do we think that perhaps everyone in the school would *defer* to the caretaker, making them a high 10? It is an interesting puzzle, which illustrates how status can shift depending on circumstances. Mostly the caretaker might be a 7, who defers to those above, but in a school emergency they might become a 10, to whom everyone would willingly defer for their own safety.

Even families have a hierarchy in terms of who defers to whom – this can sometimes shift. A man who is low status at his place of work (say a 5) might be high status in his own home (10). We can all recognize the confusion when people neglect to obey status, stepping out of line, refusing to defer. This is disruptive. In a play it can be amusing, e.g. a comic servant who tries to boss their employer. The servant is lower status, a 4, but is behaving like a 10 and treating the employer as if they were lower than a servant. A 9-year-old who disobeys in class and does not defer to their teacher's higher status is perceived as a low 4 but behaving like a 10.

Exercise: Introducing status

We line up ten chairs in a straight line facing an imaginary audience. Each person is given a playing card (numbers 1–10, ace is low, no picture cards). Using their left hand they hold it on their forehead with the number facing out, so that they cannot see the number themselves. They go around the room saying a brief hello to the others in the group. There are two tasks: (1) to find out what status is on your forehead, and (2) to let others know what status is on theirs. Finally, we get people to stand behind the chair which they think is their place in the hierarchy. There might be several people behind the same chair. Then they look at their cards to see if they are accurate. Results vary hugely.

This exercise is a great ice-breaker for a first rehearsal as it is also a game and everyone seems to enjoy it. But there is often a tendency to exaggerate behaviour in a crude way. For example, if someone is letting a 2 know that they are low status, they might be overtly rude and almost unpleasant. Or if someone is letting a 9 know that they are high status, they might behave in a fawning, false manner. I usually give out new cards and do this exercise twice and I urge them to make it more real. I encourage people to help each other discover their status more honestly, as one might do in a social situation

– to treat someone of high or low status as you might in real life. This gives everyone a chance to appreciate the subtlety.

Inner and outer status

Next I introduce the concept that we often have an inner status that differs from our outer status.

In Shakespeare's *Macbeth*, Lady Macbeth lives in a world where women have no real status. She may be perceived by the world as a low 3, virtually powerless. But her inner status might be a high 10. She longs to be a 10 in the world and could get closer to it if her husband were to rise up the ladder and become a 10 himself.

Stanley Kowalski in *A Streetcar Named Desire* might feel internally that he is a high 10 or deserves to be. But he is a factory worker from Polish immigrant stock, and knows the world sees him as a mere 5. He is aware that his wife's sister Blanche DuBois looks down on him and thinks of him as common. The tension is high when someone like Kowalski who is internally a 10 feels the world is treating him as lower status. He becomes a festering bomb seeking revenge.

Body language

An actor who was playing Macbeth was doing excellent work, but I felt that her body posture was letting her down. Macbeth in the middle of the play is a 10, but the actor had a body language of a 7. I could have addressed this by telling her she had to stand straighter, be more military, but instead I made her aware that her posture was low status and that if she could achieve a status of 10 in her body it would affect her mental state. I believe this was more helpful than being critical of her posture. I also encouraged her to practise moving and standing like a 10 in her daily life as part of her work on the role.

Another element here is Macbeth's inner status. He is so horrified and ashamed by what he has done that he might inwardly shrink to low status. Therefore he needs to push those feelings away in order to achieve his goals and hold onto power. His body achieves this by pumping up, becoming more and more 10.

Exploring status

I set up improvisations where twosomes can explore status, inner and outer. As we are exploring status I include wants, but leave obstacles out of the exercise in order to have just one point of concentration.

Exercise: Improvisation

Jane is a 10 in charge of personnel at a large department store. She is in an office sitting at a desk/table. Her task: to tell a temporary salesperson, Sean, that the store is letting him go because of reports that he is regularly late and neglects the customers. Sean is working on the men's gloves counter.

Jane's want: *To fire Sean*
Sean's want: *To keep his job*

The group watches how the improvisation changes if I vary the status of each character.

- Jane is a 10; Sean is a 3. Sean has been called in, he enters and sits. For this exercise, if Jane is playing 10 well she will be 10 inner and outer. Sean is only a 3 inner and outer, but tries to achieve his want, to keep his job. If Jane is not playing a strong enough 10, I will prompt her to do so. If Sean is too strong for a 3, I encourage him to re-enter and try again.

- I change Sean's status to an 8. We start again. It will become evident that it is much harder for Jane to dominate an 8.

- I change Jane's status to a 5. This means that she may still be seen as a 10 in the office but internally she does not feel like a 10, she feels like a 5. This makes it very hard for her to dominate an 8. I can take things further and ask Sean to be a 10. When this exercise works, the observers can see how playing with status is a powerful tool.

- I ask more twosomes to try this exercise as we try different statuses. It is particularly amusing if Sean, seen by the world as a low 3, behaves like a high 10 and I encourage him to treat Jane (10) as if she is a low 2. This calls to mind traditional comedy situations where a low status servant is stepping out of line and assuming they are in charge.

Exercise: Full company status improvisation

Here is an exercise that can be handled by a large group of people. I propose that they are all supermodels who earn vast amounts of money. I reference a supermodel agency which represents models of a variety of ages and looks. They are all high earners and the world sees them as 10s. Next, I show each one a card which shows their inner status. No one else sees this card. I give out different inner statuses. I suggest that a wealthy, successful supermodel might easily feel very low internally, might feel they have no worth except for their looks. Or another might feel like a 7 or 10 internally and would behave accordingly.

They have all been called to a casting call. They don't know each other. They don't know why they are all called at the same time. This gives them a reason to speak in the improvisation and a reason to connect.

The want: To discover why they are there while convincing each other that they are a high 10.

Afterwards we discuss what people have noticed or learned. Then sitting in a circle we go on to a group discussion, looking at various characters in the play and trying to identify their status both internal and external.

Status can be very helpful in rehearsal. Often you want a character to have more pride, to treat others with less deference, and this can be achieved simply by pointing out that they need to play higher status. It is surprising how often that can feel easily achievable. Whereas if you had said 'Try to be more proud, give them a harder time', they might find that psychologically challenging and harder to attain.

When a scene does not seem to be working, when the necessary conflict or tension is missing, it is often useful to investigate the status of the characters. Who is higher and who is lower in the scene? Are they the same status? Is one character trying to raise their status and dominate the other? Often by adjusting the status the scene will come alive in a completely different way. It is worth playing with this device to see what it yields.

In the play *Half Life* by John Mighton, Raymond Coulthard was playing Donald, who strikes up a relationship with a woman, Anna, when they are each visiting a parent in a retirement home. They meet often in the waiting area for relatives. Together Ray and I had agreed the character was an 8 in the world. He was outspoken and opinionated, so we settled on him being internally a 9. I was attending a note session with the producer who had seen a preview, and he mentioned that in reading the play he had thought Donald's character was more weedy and unconfident. I wondered if the actor and I had been mistaken. This sent me back to carefully examining the script and gradually I began to see what he meant. Donald was often self-disparaging in front of Anna, the other character.

As I knew Ray, the actor playing Donald, well, I knew him to be very confident and knowledgeable. Because we had worked together before, I felt able to discuss this even though he had a preview performance that evening. He was startled, but agreed that he would have a go at playing the character as if he were unconfident internally. So now he was still an 8 in the world, but a 5 inside. To our amazement, very early on the audience began to chuckle at the character. The audience were identifying with Donald being self-deprecating. They found it amusing. Ray was so experienced that he was immediately able to see where this was going. He went for it 100 per cent and as the laughter grew we realized that internal status had got at something essential about his character. It changed everything. The play was still very moving, but full of human warmth as well.

4

Improvisation

When I suggest to actors that we will do some improvising, I often sense a shudder of dread in the room. Why? Partly because improvisation can be an embarrassment for those attempting it and can easily deteriorate into a competition to amuse each other with clever or funny remarks. And who knows whether actors have had any training in improvisation? It is more than likely in any given rehearsal room there would be a plethora of ideas about how to improvise.

For the most part I try to run a rehearsal room where the emphasis is on 'doing', and improvisation can achieve that. Too much chat can be exhausting for everyone, and people are so keen to make their points that I am not always convinced that we really hear each other. In 1981 when Donald McWhinnie, an eminent theatre director, was directing the first production in England of *Translations* by Brian Friel, he explained to me that he always encouraged actors to talk as much as they like in the first week, just to let them get it all out. Afterwards he felt they were more open to his guidance and ideas, and therefore more able to listen to him and to each other.

Over the years I tried to use improvisation as a tool while devising or rehearsing material, but as I had no training it was at best a process of trial and error. Finally I have worked out a method which works for me, and I would like to pass on some essentials in the hope that others could find them of use, bearing in mind that these techniques might not tally with more traditional improvisation training.

Why improvise?

My use of improvisation arose from necessity, when it seemed the best way to explore certain areas of work. For example:

- To establish a character's wants/main drive through experience, rather than through chat and discussion. If possible I would do this early in rehearsal.
- To allow actors to explore the first time their characters met or underwent early formative experiences.
- To allow several characters to relive the moment of a traumatic experience that may have occurred years before the play, e.g. *The Cherry Orchard* family on the evening of the day that Ranevskaya's son drowned.
- To explore difficult choices and decisions the character is confronted with in a scene. How their wants and obstacles operate. Creating a modern equivalent scenario that allows for this.

Aims

Having watched many botched improvisations, I now start by explaining to the company why I use improvisation.

- We are improvising so that one, or sometimes two actors at a time can fully explore some aspect of character/need/want/relationship.
- The other actors are in the improvisation to assist, to play obstacles. The improvisation is not for them, they are not the main characters.
- Each person must enter the improvisation with a want/ objective/need.

Given that actors might have differing concepts about improvisation and its aims, improvisation can be confusing and a challenge. As I often have to stop the improvisation in order to prompt and coax it in a more specific direction it is important to maintain a positive, encouraging atmosphere.

Ross in Macbeth

In Chapter 3, I introduced a situation where the actor, Liam, was playing Ross in *Macbeth*. Ross, the messenger bearing news in so many scenes, is stricken and bereft when he sees his former hero, Macbeth, becoming dangerous and corrupt – a murderer who is destroying Scotland. We discussed a big want for the character. Liam's proposals for the want were weak. The big want has to be huge, it needs to exist in the character as a passionate drive. As I was failing in my efforts to get Liam to experience this want as a driving force, I turned to improvisation as a way in. Finally I suggested: *To be my country's guardian.*

How can I present this big want to the actor by moving it from Shakespeare's day to a more familiar context, so that he feels comfortable improvising? Often it helps if I search for a setting in the world of theatre, as it is a hierarchical, idealistic and familiar environment. I suggest to Liam that he is working in the marketing department of a theatre that he fears is losing its way, losing its values, bowing too easily to market pressure. I need to give him a situation where his character can play his want fully. *To be the company's guardian.* I propose that his character asks if he can attend a board meeting.

I set up the board meeting with a few people. Liam attends the meeting and presents his worries. His task/want is to convince them that the theatre is in trouble, he needs them to believe this and act upon it. In this improvisation I re-emphasize that he sees himself as the 'guardian' of the company, he *wants* to save it from losing its way. He needs to believe it is a life-and-death matter for him, that he cares so passionately about this that he would risk losing his job.

When Liam started out, he was being polite and deferential to the board members. I would stop the work and urge him to play higher status: to be firm with these people, to be aware of what is at stake and how much this theatre means to him. That it means more to him than his personal life. It took a while, quite a bit of stopping and starting. Often I need to ask 'On a scale of 1 to 100 per cent, how much do you *want* your goal?' Often the actor will admit the percentage was actually quite low. We try again. I encourage the others to present obstacles to Liam achieving his want. Finally he was operating with real authority and weight and passion. It felt like we had broken ground, but later in rehearsal it seemed Liam had completely forgotten this work and I had to repeatedly remind him to access that experience.

In this case I think it was simply that Liam had little training. If he had developed his own technique of how to tackle a role, this would not matter. Many fine actors have not trained, but have learnt their craft from others and from experience; they can function brilliantly. In Liam's case I hope that this experience opened him to a technique that would anchor his work in the future.

Improvisation for building ensemble

The Cherry Orchard by Anton Chekhov involves a large household, a cast of eleven. I was keen to give the company some early experiences to start building a true ensemble. At first we shared thoughts and research about the characters and their world, but I also wanted the actors to have an active experience. As we were early in rehearsal and did not know each other, it would be difficult to expect eleven people to improvise freely together. To make it more comfortable I suggested the improvisation would be without words, but that of course if someone wanted to speak they should feel free.

Ten years before the play begins, Ranevskaya's son Grisha drowned in the river near the cherry orchard. I set the improvisation in the evening on the day of the boy's funeral. We had a long table and a deck of cards plus various seating areas. I made sure each person in the room had a want: Anya – to rescue her mother; Ranevskaya – to survive her grief; Pischik – to distract by keeping the card game going, etc. I let it play for about ten minutes. By removing the need to speak, I was making it more possible for the actors to feel at ease and behave truthfully. And I was thankful when some felt they could speak. Time passed. There was silence. There was despair. There was wailing. There were clinging embraces. Even though we were only starting to define characters, this improvisation gave everyone a chance to imagine a shared past, to take in the other characters, to explore their responses to each other.

Afterwards we all felt drained, there was no need for a lot of discussion. The characters had been through a difficult time together. They had lived an experience that would be with them in every scene of the play.

Improvisation for establishing character

If I have a very short rehearsal period I might try in the first two days to give each actor an experience of their character in a workaday situation. In the play *Half Life* by John Mighton, Anna is visiting her father in a care home. He is suffering early dementia. She is late 30s, divorced, one child. We had little information, but we came up with a big want for her character: *She wants to love and be loved.* Her obstacles: Her marriage has failed. She is lonely. She is stricken that she is letting her father down by putting him in a home. She worries about being a good mother.

As modern plays often provide little background information on main characters, I wanted to give the actor playing Anna a sense of her daily life and how she conducts herself and meets the world. I proposed that she is being interviewed for a job designing wallpaper. She is at a table with three people interviewing her for the job. Her want for the improvisation is to convince them that she is confident and competent. I take the others to one side and tell them their task is to give her a hard time. Doubt her. Challenge her. This allows the actor to play her want against strong obstacles, inner and outer. Her want: *To get the job*. Even though it is very early days in rehearsal, it can be a valuable experience for the actor. It gives her a sense of self and most importantly it has been achieved without a lot of discussion. It also bonds the company as they are helping each other out.

You might ask why I did not set up an improvisation more connected to the play. For example, I might choose to improvise Anna talking to a friend about whether or not to put her father in a home. In that case her want could be: *I want you to help me make the decision to put my father in a home*. Her obstacle could be: *I feel guilty about putting my father away*. This choice would also be useful. However, in choosing it I would be looking at Anna's character through the lens of her play situation, whereas my emphasis is to let people first experience themselves in their daily lives, without the play's problems.

This goes back to my concern that too often we try to understand a character by how they deal with the play's issues. I cannot press too strongly the importance of exploring who that character was and what they wanted before the play's problems arose. Who were they in essence? In other words, what was their big want (or Stanislavski's super-objective)?

I hasten to add that status – one of the three essential keystones I work with – would definitely come into play for this improvisation.

- I deal with status in Chapter 3.

Exercise: Macbeth improvisation

For an actor exploring the role of Macbeth, I would set up a chance for them to experience blind ambition. This means finding a modern equivalent situation. Perhaps we imagine they are an actor who has a huge chance to prove themself if they are willing to ruin the chances of a good friend who is competing for the same role in a Hollywood film. In the play Macbeth commits murder as a step towards becoming king. This improvisation set-up might not feel as extreme as murder, but one can heighten the stakes by adding ideas. Say the friend is very vulnerable and might be destroyed emotionally were they to discover what has happened. This particular improvisation works well if one mirrors the scene in the play where Lady Macbeth and Macbeth plan to do the deed. (In this case we do not need another actor providing obstacles, as Macbeth's conscience is always there as a huge obstacle, right from the first scene.)

For Macbeth I set up the following scenario: Two young men, John and Harry, are best friends who share a flat. They are auditioning for a huge role in a Hollywood film. John is obsessively ambitious. A call comes through that both men have been invited to the final call audition. One of them will get the role. John takes the call.

Improvisation 1:

John and his girlfriend Maya are obsessed with his talent and his future. They discuss whether to tell Harry about the phone call to attend the final audition. They believe he is less talented than John. They could let Harry miss the recall. John agonizes about the decision. Maya eggs him on. They argue heatedly. He decides to cut Harry out.

Improvisation 2:

John gets the part. Months later, he has had a huge success. Harry in the meantime has had a breakdown and John feels responsible. He shares his distress and nightmares with Maya, who tries to talk him out of it, to ignore his guilt.

These improvisations allow John to explore overwhelming ambition, alongside the immediate sensation that what he is pondering horrifies him to the core of his being. It might be difficult for any actor to get in touch mentally with the idea of Macbeth's overwhelmingly huge ambition, but doing an improvisation will give them a chance to experience it. Again we are doing rather than talking.

Another example

Say an actor has to play an angry character who feels the world looks down on them, who feels their life has so far been a failure. I could set up a situation where they are in a rehearsal room where they used to be a director in training with huge promise. But because they have been too outspoken, they have now been demoted to a menial role cleaning up after rehearsals. They have to watch a rehearsal and they long to be included, to be able to participate. When they try to join in, the others, who are assisting in the improvisation by providing an obstacle, discourage and reject their efforts to participate or join in.

Improvisation – the pitfalls

- If there are several actors in the improvisation, sometimes they all talk at once. I stop the improvisation and explain that they each need to play the want I have suggested. They need to listen to each other more and only say and do things which increase the obstacle for the main character.

- I might have to stop the improvisation and say: 'You are talking too much.' I also warn them not to go off into sub-conversations with each other. They are there to provoke the main character into playing their want more strongly.

- If someone continues to be a block or disruptive in the improvisation, I would probably add restrictions or just do another version where I reduce the numbers.

- The main character goes off-piste and forgets their want or backs off how strongly they need to play it. I stop the improvisation, explain, and get them to start again, using the same situation but maybe saying: 'Let's say it is now the next day.' If I have chosen circumstances which are too complicated, or not working, I may have to say so and make adjustments.

- The actor is not keen to improvise and is subtly undermining it by inserting clever remarks. All those watching are entertained. They laugh. Often this can happen with an experienced, talented actor who is comfortable with their own process and not keen to improvise. I probably would not persist even though I believe a good improvisation would benefit them and everyone else.

I need to add that I often coach the main character from the sidelines to play their want more proactively with prompts like: 'Give her a hard time' or 'Don't let him get away with it' or 'Try to make him understand', and sometimes: 'Play your want more strongly' or 'You are playing the obstacle, go more for your want.'

Difficult actors

How to deal with an actor who is suspicious and hates games and exercises? Over the years I have learned in the first audition to mention that my rehearsal period will include games, improvisation and exercises. An actor's response to this is usually quite revealing, and I begin to get some sense of their openness or their wariness. It is reassuring if someone admits that although they have not done this sort of work, they would like to try.

When Polly Teale and I ran Shared Experience Theatre, our work was physically demanding. If we called someone back for a second audition we would arrange to have another actor present so that we could try out some physical answering exercises. These exercises were chosen because they were a good indicator of whether people would be bold and open in rehearsal.

A hopeless case

Howard was playing a lead part for me in a small company of five. Very early on it became apparent that he was intent on undermining every exercise. During an improvisation, his character announced he was going to the kitchen. Howard went behind a wall in the rehearsal room, clearly having no intention of returning during the improvisation. I wondered if this behaviour might have been provoked by embarrassment about improvising. I decided to set up a situation where no one needed to speak. The characters were sitting at a table in the evening, reading and playing cards. Howard's character choice was to fall asleep, thus undermining the exercise for the others. In most exercises Howard would make it clear with his body language that he felt we were wasting our time. The rehearsal atmosphere became unworkable and pushed me to do something I had never done before. I took Howard aside and suggested he leave the production. Howard surprised me. He insisted that although he was having difficulty, he knew he had a lot to learn and he keenly wanted to stay in the company. I was surprised. I believed him. Sadly his behaviour never changed and his attitude coloured every rehearsal. As often happens, the company managed to adapt and tolerate this disruptive presence.

Bringing the past to life through improvisation

How to approach period plays? Research into the period in which the play was written, seeking an understanding of that world, can deepen the work. It is worth remembering that although Macbeth may be set in the 1100s, Shakespeare wrote it in the early 1600s, which is a further complication. We can study the education of the day, the politics, the living conditions ... all of this is enlightening. My main desire leads me elsewhere: a desire to bring this old material alive for the present, to touch an audience with what the play means, to connect them to the play in a way which expresses its universal and timeless themes. Period research can inspire, but finally I am not intent on taking the audience on a voyage into the past.

As a director, I have rarely been required to obey period. Certainly in all my Shakespeare productions my taste has led me at most to creating a version of the period. When directing *Macbeth*, I have set it in a post-apocalyptic future – a world in which much of the detail of daily life has broken down or been destroyed. This is a freeing device as it simulates the harsh environment of the original twelfth-century Macbeth story in that it is a stripped-down world. We can invent our own details of what people wear, what they use for weapons, how they create crowns, what they use for furniture. This allows the production to concentrate on the character drives and wants, those which are timeless, which have meaning for us today .

Entering a seventeenth-century mindset: *The Heresy of Love*

Helen Edmundson's play *The Heresy of Love*, written in 2012 for the Royal Shakespeare Company, was set in a seventeenth-century Mexican convent. All the costumes and props were completely true to the period. Here was a modern writer dipping into and imagining the past. To begin with, we researched the daily lives of the period and our research led many choices in all areas of the production. However, when the company improvised or talked through scenes, I felt that we needed modern equivalents to help us. What does my character want? What are the obstacles? Using modern equivalents made it more real, easier to believe.

A modern equivalent

How can a twenty-first-century woman get close to the reality of a nun in seventeenth-century New Spain? I searched for a way to help the actors connect with their character's situation. One solution is improvisation, to give them an experience in which they deal with the character's needs, desires and obstacles. And a modern equivalent improvisation can be the most helpful. Finding that modern equivalent can be challenging.

In *The Heresy of Love*, as a writer and scholar, Juana struggles to pursue a life of the mind, but these activities are deemed to be sinful – proof that she is in league with the Devil. The Inquisition is a real presence; if Juana persists in her writing and studies, she could be expelled from her convent or, worse, imprisoned and tortured. We learned to our horror that in this repressed environment, the real Juana was made to change her handwriting because it was thought to be too masculine.

My task is to give the actor and other company members a sense of what it might be like to hunger and fight for one's freedom in such restrictive, frightening times. If I can find the adequate improvisation, it will give the company an emotionally lived experience of the times and its horrifying dangers. It will spark their inner lives.

A blind alley

My attempts to set up an improvisation among the seventeenth-century nuns in their cells, using the play and its characters as a template, were unsatisfying. The actors found it difficult to imagine themselves living as nuns in a convent in those circumstances. They resorted to clichéd conversation. This drove me to find a modern equivalent that they could relate to more honestly.

It was, as I say, challenging. I needed to provide an example of what it might be like to live in an enclosed community, cut off from the rest of the world. A community in which women are severely restricted in every aspect of their lives. The men have all the power, they make all the rules, and a woman who steps out of line in any way is in danger of her life.

A solution

Outside of rehearsal, in my head, I talked through various ideas and finally conjured up a small rural village in a distant third world country where if a woman was regularly beaten by her husband, everyone in the village would know but would all be too afraid to interfere or complain. It goes without saying this needed to be pre-mobile phones. The leaders of the village are all men. I set up the improvisation in sections. In each section I would stop and restart whenever I felt they veered off track in terms of the wants I gave each of them at the start. As I explained in Chapter 4, each actor needs to enter the scene with a specific want.

Juana becomes aware that her neighbour has been beaten by her husband.

She tells the woman she will go to the male village leaders and explain that this beating of women is wrong. That it must stop. The woman tries to stop her.

The other village women find out her intentions. I set an improvisation where they try to stop her, to make her realize the danger. But Juana refuses, she is exceptional in that she cannot abide what is happening. She needs to make a difference.

She goes to see the village leaders, the men. They frighten her because of her actions and become life-threatening. She is terrified and must make a decision.

Here is a significant moment that occurred during this improvisation. Juana was standing at a table opposite two seated male leaders, making her case about wanting to stop this beating of women. There was a pencil on the table. One of the actors picked up the pencil, held it in front of Juana's face and broke it in two. It was a terrifying moment for her and all those watching – a gesture worth a thousand words.

This improvisation became a valuable memory for all of us as we worked on the play. It felt like we had earned the right to believe in this dangerous, frightening world. And we had helped the actor playing Juana, because she had explored and had a mini-experience of Juana's impossible situation. It had helped her to connect with a character whose strong beliefs give her the courage to step out of line, even when her life is in danger. It is invaluable to have that experience through improvisation, when the words come out of your own mouth.

Developing small roles through improvisation

At the RSC we often had large casts, which was a luxury. Bear in mind that the reason for such a big company was that we were covering/understudying all the main parts with actors who were playing quite small roles. Often, I found myself at a loss because a well-meaning, talented actor had no way into their tiny role. Because they had so few lines, there was little space in rehearsal to begin to develop the character. This was hard on the actor if they had to play high status and dominate other characters in the scene.

Playing authority

In *All's Well that Ends Well*, Cliff had two tiny scenes in which his character was not our main focus, but he was in charge. He was playing the Duke of Florence, a general at war, leading his country's army. With so few lines, it was difficult for the actor to inhabit this character with any sense of need or drive or want. And especially difficult to discover a persona when there are many people in the rehearsal room, in this case about seven actors plus stage management. I needed to find a more private space for Cliff to explore character.

In most rehearsals you can carve out an hour to give real time to just one person. In this case I invited Sam, a young actor who was also playing a small part, to join the session, as I had an instinct he would bring good energy and could probably improvise well.

I needed to help Cliff find a character want through improvisation. As actors are often at a loss to find a strong want, I made a proposal. The Duke has a great desire to dominate and be seen as a powerful leader. A handy environment for an improvisation is to set up a character's workaday life. If that feels too advanced I would sometimes go back in time to when they were a teenager with demanding or difficult circumstances and perhaps longed to prove themselves to a parent or to the world.

To start off, I put Cliff into an office situation where he is the boss. Because it is a modern office, this frees the actor from having the additional task of playing a military role and bearing. In order for him to experience high status behaviour and drive I prompted him to frame the big want as: 'I want to be a powerful, inspiring leader of men.' I then gave him physical status in the space by providing a desk and a chair.

Cliff's want in the scene is: 'I want complete efficiency and to have total control over my organization.' Sam, the other actor, plays Cliff's assistant, and is bringing him typed reports. I suggest that the reports are poor. Sam is slow-moving. His behaviour is providing obstacles to Cliff's want. Cliff has to reprimand and pressurize. I encourage Cliff to express his frustration, perhaps I press him to act this out, to crumple the reports and throw them about.

Another idea: Put several chairs into the space and another table. Sam the assistant is arranging the chairs/table and papers for a special meeting with important people. This provides high stakes for both characters. Sam is inefficient and concerned. Cliff walks in and Sam is getting everything wrong. Cliff tells him off, begins to instruct him. By directing Sam to be inefficient and weak, I am putting obstacles in Cliff's way so that he has to work harder to achieve his goal of efficiency and total control. He has to use high status and inhabit a huge need to succeed.

If Cliff is still feeling weak and too amenable, I will refer back to status exercises which I did with the company in the first few days. I point out that he is playing the scene as if he is an 8, not a 10. I may have to push him to treat Sam as a 2. In order to raise the stakes, I might add that his men's lives are in danger if he as Duke of Florence is unable to control everything and everyone to a high standard. It might also be necessary to suggest to our assistant Sam (I will whisper this on the side) that he be particularly lazy or confused or recalcitrant. I could try all three if these obstacles help Cliff to become stronger and more dominating.

Most actors respond extremely well to this sort of help. They feel more confident, grounded and focused on their tasks. They are then able to bring this into the rehearsal when we revisit the scene in a crowded rehearsal room. If they seem to be leaving the work behind, I might say: 'Remember in the improvisation when you . . .' and that can usually bring them back to the same level.

Snout in *A Midsummer Night's Dream*

Here's another example. The characters in *A Midsummer Night's Dream* are putting on a play. In their band of six, three of the characters have very few lines in which to establish themselves. Yes, they are supposed to be funny and if you are lucky you manage to cast actors who will somehow find the humour. But that is not always so. Anyway I am not interested in comic business that is tacked on, I believe that comedy is funnier when it comes from character and situation.

So, how to find the base character for each of these small parts? In my production two of the actors were able to offer things in rehearsal, to build a character on their own, but Rob, playing Snout the Tinker, was clearly lost. He had no idea where to begin. I was not even sure he had a sense of comedy.

Again I did a private session with him. In Shakespeare's *Dream*, we meet Snout who has joined a little acting troupe. He is to play the part of Wall, the character whose role is to keep the lovers apart. These small characters are usually played as hapless, pathetic innocents, but I wanted something more wide-ranging. I had an idea. Let's have someone play this as a character who is quick to anger and not happy with the role he has been given. How do we build a character for Snout which will encompass this?

If the character is going to be furious and frustrated at their lack of control or a feeling of disrespect, I need to think up circumstances that will get us there. To find character in a period piece I will look for a modern equivalent so that the actor can feel familiar with the world they are improvising in. I invited my assistant Phil to be a scene partner and suggested Rob explore someone who feels a bit lost and unappreciated in life. We did improvisations where he is seen as a failure in school. His big want: 'I want to be admired and respected.' In terms of status (see Chapter 3) the world would see him as a low 3, but he wants to be a high 10. So there is inner pride and outer humiliation at work. He joins a drama troupe run by Phil and gradually develops a passionate desire to get into drama school and become an actor. The troupe is doing a play. He is not happy about having such a small part. In one improvisation he tries to talk Phil into letting him have a bigger role. He is refused. He tries harder and is refused again. Finally he becomes morose.

When Rob rejoined the main rehearsal, I could see that in the early scenes where Snout has little to say, he was more rooted as a person and fully present with the other characters. He was concentrating on his character's *want* – to gain experience and have a real future as an actor. He *wanted* to learn from the others, to fit in. In later scenes when he was playing Wall, he became frustrated and annoyed because the others were pushing him around. Finally this became extremely funny and thankfully it felt very real.

Through improvisation, we had together quickly sketched in a character who has a strong want and obstacles. When this works, it gives the actor a beginning, a base to build on. It also becomes a baseline you can refer and hold on to. If the actor suddenly goes off-piste and becomes vague or brings a different persona to the rehearsal room, you can feel justified in referring to the work you did together. As the leader/guide for the production, you can firmly insist on a return to that work, those earlier decisions.

Using the world of theatre as a setting for improvisation

In looking for equivalents which will be a spark for the actor, I often propose a theatre situation. The theatre world will be immediately familiar to the company. It is hierarchical, a world in itself, so it provides an instant environment for exploring status, power, desire, rejection, fear, love, etc.

The Tempest

Shakespeare's *The Tempest* is set in a strange, magical world far from all civilization. In rehearsal I set modern improvisations where Prospero is the artistic director of a theatre company in a remote area of Scotland. Ariel is a female choreographer who has become his muse, inspiring his most remarkable creations.

She longs to be free, to be her own person and make her own work. These improvisations were a fruitful way to explore the emotions in their fraught relationship and it was particularly resonant in that moment late in the play when Prospero gives Ariel her freedom. We used this theatre scenario to explore many other moments or relationships in *The Tempest*.

5

Rehearsal process

I believe that we the audience are most engaged with actors when they reveal themselves through the medium of a character. At heart, acting is a baring of the soul and an audience knows when this occurs. They can sense when the playing is truthful, and they will then feel an emotional pull toward the actor and the character. Actors are able to articulate feelings which the audience understands but can't name.

You may point out, however, that we the audience don't always agree about when this takes place. We have different taste in actors: some touch us, some do not. But for me a commitment to using the self as a starting point is essential to the work. And my role is to guide the actor towards a deep emotional understanding of what makes their character tick. Perhaps this is why I turn to improvisation whenever I sense an actor is not personally engaged with the part they are playing. By creating an improvisation that sets up a modern-day parallel to their character's needs, I can give them an experience close to their own lives. Hopefully this makes the situation in the play more real for them.

Fielding the chaos

Actors often feel powerless and therefore it can be confusing for a company when I invite an open collaboration in the rehearsal room. Where is the power? Who is in charge?

Without me being aware, the actors can begin to think all my searching and posing of questions might indicate that I am lost in a morass of indecision.

Occasionally an actor I have worked with previously has come to me at the end of a rehearsal day and alerted me to a growing sense of insecurity amongst the cast, as if they fear there is no one at the helm. I have learned the best way to deal with this is to call the company together and explain that I am definitely going to make the final decisions. I tell them I want to keep the process open, that the work is stronger when everyone feels free to make suggestions and, most importantly, to try things without worrying about a finished product. But finally, I assure them, I will make the choices, I shall act as the tastemaker.

Tastemaker defined

Tastemaker is an awkward word and might seem a frivolous choice, but it comes from a special time in the 1970s at Hampstead Theatre, when I was directing the great actor Ian Holm as Astrov in Chekhov's *Uncle Vanya*. Widely known in film for his roles in *Chariots of Fire* and *Aliens*, Holm's stage work was stunning and a seminal inspiration to so many of us. His Henry V and Richard III at the Royal Shakespeare Company will be forever embedded in my brain.

When I found myself directing Holm in *Uncle Vanya* I was naturally incredibly nervous. After all, here was someone I had perceived as a god of the theatre. Fortunately Ian Holm's work ethic was open and curious and as the challenge of Chekhov's great play became the focus in the rehearsal room, working with him became comfortable and creative. He would often say that he could offer ten ways of playing a scene, but that it was up to me to guide and decide: 'You are the tastemaker.' Mind you, he was by no means typical. I am not sure many actors would feel that confident and offer so many options, but it was encouraging that he expected me to lead and that he trusted me and was happy to endow me with the role of 'tastemaker'.

Troubleshooting with actors

Learning the best approach for each actor takes time, is not always achievable, and I don't always manage it. Whereas some actors have a rich working technique and can get on independently, working on their own or in tandem with the director to find their way to a performance, others are more needy. Maybe they always start out fearful and lacking in confidence. This can be worrying for a director. But perhaps the same actor can produce splendid work if the director is sympathetic and nurturing. When I work with that actor a second time I will know they need space in the beginning to flounder, and I will not push them too hard too early. I will know from experience that they will get there eventually.

Another actor might be avoiding the necessity to dig deep and question and challenge themselves. There can be any number of reasons why this is happening. Fear? Apparent arrogance? Here I may choose to be more forceful and demanding. It is worth a try and will soon become obvious whether that is a helpful approach or whether it makes things worse!

What about an actor who is subtly undermining me as director? If it is subtle, it might take me a while to recognize what is happening. It might take the form of remarks such as 'Oh really, I thought I was already doing that', or 'Sorry, but that seems very obvious'. Looking back, I know that I have often addressed this problem too late in the day, after this actor has wasted everyone's time. It basically needs a one-to-one talk in a private space when I would ask the actor if there was a problem. And then perhaps tell them outright that it felt like we were pulling against each other. Sometimes – and I hasten to repeat, sometimes – this can make a big difference in the room. But not always.

Power struggle

Finally I think I should mention a power struggle – when an actor is not willing to try my suggested way into a scene. They might have a go at cooperating, but as soon as we start on the floor I can see they are not working with my prompts. They infer that my ideas are naff or pointless.

Here is an example: A leading actor was playing a complex character who has experienced a devastating comeuppance. He has been exposed and suffered public humiliation. He has to enter a public space where many people are watching him. As sometimes happens in rehearsal, an idea popped into my head, as ideas often do, appearing as if from nowhere. I suggested to him that his character smile on entrance and keep smiling as he spoke. He questioned 'why' and I could only say 'I don't know, but it's worth a try'. Perhaps I was thinking of a sheepish grin when someone has made a fool of themselves. Previously, this actor had been reluctant to take my lead, ignoring my prompts or suggestions. But for once he tried my idea and I was aware that he could see it was working well, it made sense to him. Hopefully this was a step towards a collaboration.

The worst thing about being in a power struggle with an actor is that you find yourself passionately fighting for and defending something you want to try out. This becomes counterproductive because the best explorations happen when you explore things just for the heck of it. If you have to fight for what was only a glimmer of an idea, you are caught in the trap of trying to prove that you are right. It negates any sense that this is a place to try out, investigate and explore. A place to recognize that some ideas are not working. I am glad to say this sort of director/actor struggle does not happen often, but when it does, it is a drain on everyone's energy.

In my experience, actors who are resistant or who give the director a hard time or who are time-consuming will eventually acquire a reputation for being 'difficult'. Obviously it can have a major effect on their career, and they will be cast less and less. Sadly, many of these actors are hugely talented and have a great deal to offer. But if their 'process' is too demanding, they can fall by the wayside.

One step at a time

If I were to hand on one piece of advice, it would be to progress a rehearsal one suggestion at a time. I cannot place too high a value on this. While I am watching a scene I may see many things which could be improved. For example:

- Play the want more, have more effect on the other character.
- Play the obstacle more, feel it bubbling away under the surface and bursting out.
- Take more time to take each other in.
- Play higher (or lower) status.
- See if you can work in a lower voice register.
- What happens if you look at each other less?

The list could be endless. The temptation is to share all of this with the actor. However I firmly believe people can only take in one idea at a time. If I mention five things which need addressing, how can the actor possibly concentrate on all of them while they have another go at the scene? Their head would be reeling with director's notes, there would be no space for the character's thoughts. For me the major challenge is to decide on the spot which one thing I will start with. Which of my suggestions will be most important at this time and which can wait? Which one will possibly move the work forward? It's about finding the right prompt at the right time.

Over the years I became more confirmed in this approach. My discussions with voice and Pilates teachers confirmed that when you make a correction on a person's voice or body they need to go through a process:

First – they need to become aware in the body of the point you are making.
Second – they have to consciously address it as they work.
Third – it will become natural, without them having to consciously think about it.

This physical/mental process takes time and it makes sense. A good teacher would limit themselves to one or two points at a time. Similarly the actor can take my single suggestion and go into the scene again with just one challenge in mind. Afterwards we can discuss whether or not they managed to take this on board. If not, perhaps we try again. This keeps the rehearsal on track and hopefully avoids endless conversation and discussion around myriad aspects of the character and the scene. However, if an actor appears to be stuck and unable to move forward, I might move on to improvisation as a way in.

Scheduling

Every director will develop their favoured way of scheduling rehearsal. Because I usually find rehearsal times too short and therefore pressured, I plan each day meticulously in order to gain precious time. Ideally one would map out a schedule for each week, but in my case that schedule seems to need constant adjustment. As the rehearsal day develops, I may become aware that an actor or a scene is going to need extra time, which means rethinking the next day's call. This can be stressful and in the best situations a stage manager will come to my rescue, catching me in the afternoon tea break and helping me to make quick decisions to create the next day's call.

Script map

In my desire to have a physical picture of the play and all its elements, I have devised script maps. They make it possible to see the whole play laid out. A script map is a breakdown of each section that can have its own rehearsal. It means at a glance I can see where the songs, where the twosomes, where the solo speeches, where the fights are. It becomes extremely useful for planning a rehearsal day, particularly if I am accommodating actors being out of the room for voice work or fittings or personal issues. A spare half-hour can be filled by looking at the script map, which is virtually a menu of scenes or elements to choose from.

> • At the end of this chapter you will find a partial script map for *King Lear.*

Warming up

How important are physical and vocal warm-ups? In the late 1960s when I first began working in fringe theatre, we were exploring what felt like new territory, perceiving the actor as the centre of the work. The power of the actor's physical presence became primary and this meant a commitment to developing their physical and vocal range. For this to happen we needed daily training. Daily warm-ups then led naturally to a warm-up before each performance. It is worth noting that while we on the fringe were committed to this tuning of the actor's instrument, it was not the norm for conventional theatre companies.

Stephen Rea

The inspiring Stephen Rea left his native Belfast in the late 1960s. He was a young actor looking to make his way in London theatre when he came across my company, Freehold. Our rigorous exercises and our vocal warm-ups were completely foreign to Stephen, but he was attracted to working in an alternative, non-established way and so he threw himself into the process.

As the years went by Stephen has remained passionately faithful to that way of working and reminds me that when he was working in places like the Old Vic, there were times when he would find himself the only actor onstage before a show who was actually doing a warm-up. In fact he was such a curiosity that the ushers used to make a special effort to come and watch him.

As conventional theatre began to mimic and absorb the highly physical and vocal expressiveness they were seeing in fringe work, established companies began to make space for voice and movement teachers. They have become essential to many rehearsal processes. And of course that means warm-ups have become the norm.

Warm-up as part of the rehearsal day

In some cases, directors arrange to have a physical and vocal warm-up to start each day. This works perfectly well if you are a director who prefers to have the entire company present throughout the rehearsal day. Alternatively one can schedule weekly half-hour warm-ups for the whole company together.

In my case, the rehearsal schedule varies from day to day. So at the start of the day I will lead a ten-minute stretch and warm-up for the first people who are called. Ideally if there is a second room I call actors who are scheduled to rehearse later to a self-directed warm-up in that room. There is no doubt that it makes a difference rehearsing with an actor who has warmed up their instrument, just as one would expect of a musician preparing to play.

Blocking

Traditionally, years ago when rehearsal periods were extremely short, mapping out each actor's movement and placing in each scene was probably a necessity. It was a quick, efficient way for an actor/manager to get the play on its feet and in some kind of satisfying shape. In the nineteenth century, once play directors emerged, they took over the blocking, aka moves. There is a joke that directors need to block the show in order to prevent the actors bumping into the furniture. And in a short rehearsal period, it makes complete sense to work in this way.

Historically, once rehearsal times became more extended, there was less need to pin everything down at an early stage. The rehearsal could be a more open place for exploration and 'trying things out'. In my case, blocking becomes a main tool in creating the stage pictures which tell the emotional story. For this reason I ponder endlessly the placing of furniture. I have these positions marked and held to whenever the show moves to another venue. For me, at any moment, the stage image and the people in it are like a painting full of detail and emotional cues. Each movement takes the story forward or shifts emphasis. My favoured approach during rehearsals is to leave the actors free to move as they will, but gradually as my gut feelings about how to transmit the story become stronger, I will be more and more specific about where and when they move, paying close attention to how the space is being used. This is of course a highly personal way of working. Each director finds their own way.

Notes from the writer

Notes from the writer can be disconcerting. Perhaps the writer is doubtful a certain actor is sufficient in the role. I might need to reassure that we are still in a rehearsal process and all will be well. Of course, if the writer points out aspects of a scene which I have been missing, it can be a big help for the next rehearsal. I also go back to the script and if I feel that what the writer wants is not in the scene, then I would point this out and suggest a rewrite.

Run-throughs

Rehearsal periods vary in length, but whatever the period I would always aim for a run-through, often called a stagger-through, for the last rehearsal day in the penultimate week. This gives the actors a weekend to realize how up-to-date they are on line learning and to gear themselves for the final push.

In the last rehearsal week I would try to schedule several run-throughs before the final run. If the play is a long one and time is short, I might have to resort to running large chunks rather than the whole play. Run-throughs can often solve a lot of issues; things fall into place as the run encourages the actors to take more responsibility for making decisions and maintaining the work they have experienced during rehearsals.

Receiving and processing notes

Once you are into run-throughs, you may be getting notes from the producer or director of the theatre. When a director gets notes, they are in a vulnerable place. If the notes come from a reliable source, someone I have come to trust, I want to be open-minded and accepting of criticism. But this can be dangerous. Yes, I want to be open, but I have learned the importance of giving myself time and space for evaluating notes. I need to take them seriously, but then I also need a chance to absorb and ponder, only taking on the suggestions which make sense to me.

Rewrites during previews

The writer, director and producer will learn a great deal from preview performances before the opening night when the critics come. It is inevitable that the pressure will be on for rewrites, sometimes from the producer and director, sometimes from the writer themself.

This is a delicate time. And if there are very few previews, changes are going to be stressful for everyone, particularly the actors who have to learn new material and then perform it that night. Passionate conversations take place with all concerned about what is needed. And here is something vital I have learned and need to keep reminding myself: Yes, people can sense when something is not working, but their ideas of how to fix it can vary hugely. The trick is to keep your head and find your way through the many suggestions coming your way. The diagnosis might be right but the remedy wrong.

Disagreement needs to be negotiated diplomatically if possible. And it is worth remembering that the writer often has a contractual right to have the deciding vote, the last word.

Opening night nerves

I rarely come away from an opening night performance, especially one full of critics, where I feel satisfied with the outcome. Opening night nerves are sure to affect some of the cast, and one will occasionally see actors lose their way in an excess of emotion or a spate of what one can only call 'overacting'. Is there a strategy for preparing the actors? I used to encourage them to hold fast to the work they had developed and not be distracted by the presence of critics. But eventually I came to think it would be better to avoid talking about critics at all.

Instead I openly acknowledge that there will be many distractions on the night, particularly friends and relatives. Therefore the important thing is to concentrate on the story we have to tell. I remind them that now they are the owners of the story, they know from the inside how it works. They are the storytellers who can take the audience on a journey. And then I give them a task, a challenge: When you come off stage after any scene, your one concern should be whether you made the scene work for your scene partners. And if your character is talking to the audience, then the audience is your scene partner. Did you affect them with your purpose? Basically I am going back to my first premise about how to lose self-consciousness. If you have a task, it frees you. And my hope is that this focus helps them to concentrate on their wants and drives, the tools which will connect them to each other and then to the audience.

Partial script map for *King Lear*

(Movement sequences are in CAPS. The numbers are page numbers. Each item can be rehearsed on its own.)

ACT ONE

Prologue

Act 1, Scene 1 Lear's Palace
1. Kent and Gloucester and Edmund
2. Lear divides the kingdom
CORDELIA STRIPPED
PAPERS THROWN
KENT BANISHED
7. France and Burgundy are offered to Cordelia
9. Cordelia's farewell to sisters
10. Regan and Goneril make plans

Act 1, Scene 2 Gloucester's House
INTRO GLOUCESTER AND EDGAR
11. Edmund: solo 'legitimate'
12. Edmund/Gloucester: 'What paper were you reading?'
14. Edmund: solo 'foppery of the world'
14. First Edgar scene – Edmund warns Edgar he is in great danger

Act 1, Scene 3 Goneril's Palace
16. Goneril instructs Oswald and others to disrespect Lear

Act 1, Scene 4 Goneril's Palace
17. Solo: Kent takes on disguise
17. Lear takes on Kent
18. Lear and Knights demand dinner; Lear strikes Oswald
21. First Fool
26. Goneril/Lear conflict: '50 of my followers'
25. PLUS Albany – milky gentleness
28. Goneril sends letter to Regan via Oswald

Act 1, Scene 5 Goneril's Palace
29. Lear gives letters to Kent for delivery to Regan
29. Lear and Fool: 'I did her wrong'

SEE OSWALD AND KENT EACH RUNNING WITH
LETTERS

6

The mystery of comedy

In 1979 I directed *The Tax Exile* at the Bush Theatre, then a tiny space over a pub in London's Shepherd's Bush. We had a terrific response for this brilliant farce by Jonathan Gems (son of Pam Gems) with the comedy firing on all cylinders. After the show opened, I attended a performance, and was astonished to see how much of the comic response was fading. The cast were despondent. I spoke to them about truthfulness and encouraged them to think less about getting laughs and more about playing their characters' needs. Then, I suggested, the comedy might return. And it did.

The source

It has been said that comedy is much more difficult to play than tragedy. And conversely it is also true that there are countless examples of comedians being brilliant at tragedy, moving us deeply in dramatic roles. But the opposite is less common, and many a dramatic actor has had a difficult time attempting comedy.

Where does the essence of comedy, of funniness originate? Can we pin it down? Define it? Endless theories about humour and its source have been researched, numerous essays have been written. How many times have I heard directors and actors remark that comedy is deadly serious? I agree. In my experience the truest route to playing comedy is to begin by taking it seriously.

Comedy derived from optimism

I made a major discovery about one aspect of comedy on my first professional directing job, a musical called *The Fantasticks*. The character of Henry is a Shakespearean actor, ancient and extremely short-sighted. His eyesight is so poor that he continually bumps into things, talking into thin air when he fails to notice that someone he is addressing has moved to another position onstage. I knew this character was supposed to be funny, and my actor had been funny in past comedy roles, but in rehearsal he was not amusing. I kept asking myself why? Eventually I had an idea that might be worth pursuing. Perhaps we were not amused because his situation was so sad, really quite tragic. But we would laugh if he were full of optimism, if he held onto a positive attitude even though he was constantly being thwarted. Think Charlie Chaplin or Laurel and Hardy. I shared these thoughts with the actor and we tried this approach, finally arriving at the comedy in the character.

An exercise in understanding optimism

Years later this understanding about optimism was supported when I had the good fortune to be in a workshop with teacher and theatre archivist Peter Hulton. We looked at how a simple activity could start off completely serious and straightforward and then grow into comedy.

A man is trying for the first time to do up a tie in a proper knot. He keeps getting it wrong. He gets frustrated and angry and pulls at the tie while trying to do it up. He throws it on the

*floor and stamps on it. The situation is becoming tragic, his
frustration is driving him wild, he can't cope. He tries again.*

This is not funny. Why? Because he is totally pessimistic about
ever achieving success. His pessimism is driving him towards a
loss of self-belief, towards victimhood. What would make it
funny? Optimism. If you say to the actor: 'Carry on trying to
achieve your goal, keep getting it wrong, but do it with
complete optimism, total positive thinking. You are sure you
can make it work if you simply persist and keep trying new
approaches to tying the tie.' This is the essence of clowning –
again, think Charlie Chaplin. If the actor has any of that
mysterious thing we call 'a sense of comedy' it will become
funny.

There are good examples of this in Alan Ayckbourn's plays.
His characters are often in extremely depressing situations and
yet they amuse us. Once again I believe the element of optimism
is at work. The characters are in a challenging situation, but
they go to extraordinary lengths to surmount difficulty – such
extreme and convoluted lengths that their situation becomes
ridiculous and finally funny.

In Ayckbourn's play *Absurd Person Singular*, Jane and
Sidney are entertaining Ronald, an important banker, and his
wife. They are frantic and desperate for everything to be
perfect. Outdoors it is raining. When they realize they have run
out of tonic water, Jane goes out of the back door in her
husband's raincoat and hat to go to the shops. On her return
Jane is locked out of the back door so has to enter by the front
door. She rings the bell. Ronald, the banker, answers the door.
In her raincoat and hat disguise, Jane dashes past Ronald
heading for the kitchen. Her husband lies to Ronald, saying
that the person in the raincoat and hat was a delivery man
bringing tonic water. We the audience roar with laughter. Jane
and Sidney's need to be perfect is desperate. But they remain
optimistic. They never give up or become discouraged. It
becomes funny when they go to extreme lengths and resort to
absurd lies in order to achieve perfection.

Case study

Taking it seriously in *The Comedy of Errors*

In 2005 I directed this wonderful play for the RSC. It follows the story of two sets of identical twins separated at birth. The play has all the elements of farce and commedia dell'arte: mistaken identity, slapstick beatings, false accusations, etc. A cornucopia of comic business is in order and productions of *The Comedy of Errors* can become a free-for-all of comic invention; anything goes if it produces a laugh. But since I don't believe I am being true to the writing unless the comedy comes from the text itself, from character and situation, for me this is problematic. Of course actors can invent and perform funny stage business to add to the fun, but there is something askew when the comedy is tacked on. I prefer to embrace the challenge and ferret out the serious underbelly of the story. Once this is discovered, one can begin to build the comedy in a truthful and organic way.

Shakespeare leads the way on this. He teaches us the importance of the weighty life-and-death situations necessary for comedy. In each of his comedies, the first scene brings in characters who are in tragic or life-threatening situations. For example, in *A Midsummer Night's Dream*, young Hermia is threatened with death if she fails to marry her father's choice of husband. In *Twelfth Night*, Viola has narrowly survived a shipwreck and landed desolate and penniless in a foreign country. In *The Comedy of Errors*, the elderly Egeon is arrested for illegally entering Ephesus. He is given just one day, until sunset, to raise the huge fee that would free him from a certain death sentence.

Mining the text

In the process of scouring the text, looking for clues I became interested in Shakespeare's choice of Ephesus for his setting.

Historically the ancient city of Ephesus was a notorious hotbed of sorcery and witchcraft. A place of magic where there were frequent attempts to harness supernatural powers in order to cast out demons. In the first act, Shakespeare sets the scene accordingly. Antipholus of Syracuse tells the audience:

Antipholus: Act 1, Scene 2

They say this town is full of cozenage,
As, nimble jugglers that deceive the eye,
Dark-working sorcerers that change the mind,
Soul-killing witches that deform the body.
Disguised cheaters, prating mountebanks,
And many such-like liberties of sin:
If it prove so, I will be gone the sooner.

Shakespeare presents this setting very early in the play. As the designer Katrina Lindsay and I sought to create a street life world that would encompass jugglers, sorcerers, cheaters and witches capable of killing the soul, this speech became an essential keystone to the production. I was especially taken with the mention of 'prating mountebanks' and discovered the word 'mountebank' means standing on a bench or hill. This was an impetus for giving full weight to the character of Dr Pinch, who arrives late in the play to exorcize a demon. As he is a doctor I imagined he was one of Shakespeare's 'prating mountebanks', a preacher 'on a bank' who stands above the crowd selling charms and medicines.

I found a way to visually introduce the audience to Dr Pinch and this street life as the piece began. We created a non-speaking prologue where Dr Pinch comes to town with his cart full of medicines and begins to demonstrate his wares to the public.

When Shakespeare chose Ephesus as his setting he was choosing a dangerous environment. Hence Antipholus plans initially to get away from the town as soon as possible. Of course, as the story becomes more complicated, his plans go awry.

Plot

As the story of *The Comedy of Errors* unfolds, we meet Antipholus of Syracuse and his servant Dromio. They arrive in the town of Ephesus on a quest. Antipholus has been travelling the world for years searching for another Antipholus, his lost twin. In fact Antipholus has taken on the name of his lost brother as he will not feel complete until he finds him:

Antipholus: Act 1, Scene 2

I to the world am like a drop of water
That in the ocean seeks another drop
Who, failing there to find his fellow forth –
Unseen, inquisitive – confounds himself.
So I, to find a mother and a brother,
In quest of them, unhappy, lose myself.

I was struck by this short speech spoken to the audience, which introduces us to a character who would fit easily into a tragedy. Antipholus knows that he and his twin were separated in infancy. He is depressed and searching the world to find this brother who will make him complete. Here is a hero whose story might be appropriate to a serious drama. Shakespeare was certainly giving his comedy a serious underbelly.

The madcap comedy begins when the audience realizes that the identical duo of lost twin and servant are actually living in the town of Ephesus. Shakespeare puts the cherry on the cake by giving this Ephesus set of twins the same names. So now we have Antipholus and Dromio of Syracuse exploring the town and narrowly missing Antipholus and Dromio of Ephesus. Insane mistaken identity ensues.

Impact of casting on the comedy

The big decision for any director about to direct *The Comedy of Errors* will be how to cast the twins. There is a fashion for having each Antipholus also play his own twin. This can be great fun for the audience, enjoying the impressive dexterity as an actor plays identical brothers with very different personalities. But at the play's end this device becomes awkward, especially in the very moving reconciliation scene where the brothers meet and are reunited with their lost parents. With each actor playing their own twin, this has to be handled through trimming lines, mirrors and some clever stagecraft, but there is a high cost: a loss of emotion. We do not get the full power of the magical and moving moment when the brothers meet and recognize each other face to face.

When I decided to have two different actors play the twins, I was rejecting the popular choice of having one actor play himself and his own twin. Briefly, I will admit, I felt insecure about my choice. Was I just taking an old-fashioned route? Was I shying away from a lot of potential humour? But the more I read the play, the keener I was to take it seriously and explore its underlying emotional journeys. Of course an audience would be excited at the cleverness of one person playing two. But I believe that turns the play into a spectacle, pure entertainment that requires no emotional investment. It is an approach that neglects what the play is about.

If I was committed to finding the heart and soul of the piece, I needed to take on board two contrasting dramatic stories. What it means to have lost your other half, to feel your life has no meaning unless you can find him. And in contrast, the story of a brother unconsciously riddled with self-doubt, knowing he is an orphan, but having no idea of his origins or whether his parents are alive. I wanted to follow through on these stories of lost souls who eventually find each other.

Following through

It might seem like taking the play so seriously would ultimately kill the comedy. But experience has taught me that all comedy thrives on its serious base. This encouraged me to pursue the truth of the characters. As I investigated the text I began to appreciate how different the world-wandering Antipholus of

Syracuse was to his twin Antipholus of Ephesus. We learn that the infant twins and their servants were separated when their ship was split asunder in a storm. One twin, Antipholus of Syracuse, was saved by his father and grew up feeling incomplete, knowing he had lost his twin. Now he was searching the world for his other half. The other twin, Antipholus of Ephesus, had grown up never knowing his past or that he was a twin. He had been rescued by sailors, adopted by a famous warrior duke, brought up in Ephesus and had married the governor's daughter. Now he had achieved very high status.

Imagine how exciting to find these nuggets of information in the text and tune in to this phenomenon. In life, when twins are separated at birth, they are usually unaware they have a twin. But Shakespeare has done something dramatic here. One twin knows he has lost a brother, the other does not. Given these circumstances, no wonder their personalities are diametrically opposed. From clues in the text the Syracuse Antipholus comes across as a poetic, soulful young man. Not only does he possess an innate gentleness, but his relationship with his servant Dromio is often companionable and affecting. He explains that Dromio lifts his spirits when he is depressed or feeling low.

Antipholus of Syracuse (about his servant Dromio) Act 1, Scene 2

A trusty villain, sir, that very oft,
When I am dull with care and melancholy,
Lightens my humour with his merry jests.

Meanwhile his brother, Antipholus of Ephesus, presents as brash and short-tempered. We learn early on that he is rarely at home and is cheating on his wife. Through his success as a soldier, he has become important and high-ranking and is now married to the governor's daughter. I began to think of him as someone who feels insecure about who he is and whether he deserves such high rank. This insecurity has led to him behaving badly to his wife and being cruel to his servant. He needs to feel in control but is unsure of his origins and becomes aggressive and uncaring with it.

The brothers were emerging from the text as very different characters, to be explored and fleshed out in rehearsal. Once their characters were firmly grounded, the comedy in the script could be explored and, more importantly, the comedy would come from the text.

Discovering differences in the script made the brothers more than comic figures. They were real people with passionate issues. In rehearsal I went on to investigate serious back stories with each character, often using improvisation in order to root them in real needs and desires.

Improvisation

To explore the relationship between Antipholus of Syracuse and his servant Dromio, I took my lead from Antipholus explaining to a merchant that when he felt low and melancholy his servant often cheered him up with merry jests. I set a modern-day improvisation where they were a travelling salesman and his assistant in a hotel room. The salesman is depressed, too sad to go out on the town. I asked the assistant to try to cheer him up by making him laugh. The actors took this improvisation seriously. Cheering up a depressed person and trying to get them to laugh is a tall order. As they improvised this situation, it meant they had shared their relationship and experience in a believable way, which helped them to feel bonded as a pair.

In rehearsal I continued to set up improvisations so that actors could explore their characters' needs and desires in a real and honest way. Happily our search for truth grew into a hilarious evening. The *Sunday Times* wrote 'the auditorium rings with spontaneous guffaws and bursts of applause, the reward for inventive slapstick, comic precision and the timeless joy of watching people confounded by the unpredictability of life'.

Why is it funny?

Now you may ask, where does the comedy come in? Once you have dredged the text for the drama, how do you get to the funny side? Well, there are a few keystones I have described which open dramatic situations to their humorous side, one being the importance of optimism when a character faces obstacles. But, to be brutally frank, there is one major factor: you need to cast an actor who can play comedy and has a sense of timing. A tall order perhaps? Here are some suggestions for casting and playing comedy, and some of the tools I bring into the rehearsal room for transforming the dramatic into the hilarious.

Casting a funny actor

Comedy is so elusive. When you are casting, how do you know if someone is funny? If an actor reads from the text in audition and makes you smile, that may be a pretty reliable indicator. But if you yourself are the person reading the comedy scene with the actor, it might be hard to evaluate. And if the actor is reading opposite a casting director, let's face it, that is not conducive to bringing out the humour. In addition, what if the text is too sparse to give an adequate idea? Nowadays you might be casting an actor by watching a self tape, but here again this might not show off their comic sense to the best advantage.

Ideally you would be considering this actor because they have auditioned brilliantly, or are known to be funny, or you have seen them in performance. But finally, casting for comedy is going to be deeply subjective. If I were casting an actor whose work was not known to me, in a small role with very little text, I might set a simple exercise to see if they possessed that mysterious thing – 'a sense of comedy'.

Example: I say to the actor: 'Imagine that you work behind the scenes in an amateur theatre company. A performer has suddenly been taken ill and you have to make an announcement to the audience (us) explaining that the performance will be delayed for several minutes. You enter from the wings. You are extremely nervous, terrified. You make the announcement. You exit to the wings. You come back again to cancel the show. You exit again.'

This exercise can be revealing about an actor's comic sense. If the actor makes you giggle or smile, you may have the confidence to give them the part.

Chasing the laugh

Comedy can come from many places. Verbal wit, satire, mockery . . . the categories are numerous. And we who work in the theatre can tie ourselves in knots trying to understand its roots, its mechanisms, so that we can make it happen on demand. But when we try too hard, it becomes a fool's errand. Comedy's secret escapes us.

Example: At Shared Experience we were touring *Anna Karenina* for a second time, with a new cast. The lead actor was one of the few in the company remaining from the original production. He had a scene with a young woman who had a line which always got a huge laugh on the first tour. In our new production, the young woman failed to get this laugh and our lead player was convinced she would get the laugh if he coached her. This included notes on intonation: 'Go up at the end of the line'; timing: 'Wait a bit before you say it'; physicality: 'Make sure you are completely still as you say it'. Doubtless there were countless other suggestions. Needless to say, this mysterious laugh evaded all attempts to recapture it.

Where did the laugh go?

A comedy was playing in London's West End. One of its funniest scenes began to lose its laughs and the actors began to spend more and more time in offstage discussion in the dressing room, trying to identify why it had happened. As the run went on and various strategies were tried, the scene lost more and more laughs. Clearly the actors' tensions were having a negative effect. Meanwhile another scene in the play which had not been particularly funny began to get more laughs. Mystery unsolved. The gods of comedy were having a wonderful time with this group of actors.

Comedy in a small theatre space

Whenever I direct a comedy to play in a small theatre, I warn the company that the size of the 'house' will affect laughter. In a theatre with a small number of seats, the audience response is bound to differ from performance to performance. Audiences can warm to the comedy if they catch it from each other, but often those in a small audience are quiet, smiling but less inclined to laugh out loud. In order to get the laughter going, you need a few people who will laugh outright and then it might spread.

Perhaps that's why we talk about 'letting the audience know' they are watching a comedy, giving them permission to laugh. In fact some people are fond of the producer's laugh. This is a strategy where the producer or the theatre director or a helpful friend is sitting in the audience and chuckling aloud at every opportunity. It sounds mad, but it can sometimes get an audience going.

Give them a clue

As a student I attended a lecture by Hal Prince, the original producer of *A Funny Thing Happened on the Way to the Forum*, a musical derived from Plautus' ancient Roman comedy. He told us that despite its name, the show was not getting a comedy response when it was playing on tour. Possibly the audience was put off by actors in togas and intimidated by references to Roman history, not wanting to be disrespectful. On tour, as the show was being developed, the producers and director were making daily changes and someone suggested they put in an opening song called 'A Comedy Tonight'. They did. It worked. The audience had been invited to laugh; they had been given permission.

Learning from the actor

In 1981 I was directing *Who's Afraid of Virginia Woolf?* at the National Theatre with Paul Eddington playing George. Paul was a consummate comedian, having made a big impact on television in *Yes, Minister* as part of a legendary comedy double act with Nigel Hawthorne. As we got into final rehearsals, my assistant director took me aside and advised me that Eddington's performance would be killing the comedy because he was so slow on his cues. At first I was startled – the assistant director might be right. After all, being tight on cues, responding immediately to each other, is usually so vital for keeping the energy of a piece flowing.

Eddington was definitely slow on cues. Yes, he was hilarious on television, but that was a different medium, the timing would be so different. I began to worry and wondered if I needed to address this issue with Eddington before it was too late for him to adjust. But something stopped me, made me doubt this advice. I told my assistant that I was going to hold off as I knew Eddington to be a brilliant comedian and therefore it might be safest to wait until the previews and see how things went. Surely, I thought, someone who had in the past been extremely funny could be trusted regarding comic timing. I am glad to say I was proved right. Eddington's gift for comedy flourished in front of the audience and reigned supreme. Clearly I was relieved that I had not overreacted, but given myself time to trust my own judgement. Phew.

Paul Eddington's prowess impressed me even further when he explained to me that his goal in a comedy was to learn how little he needed to do and still get the laugh. Although I often watched his performance as George in Edward Albee's play, I was never any closer to understanding his comic mastery. Its mystery survives.

7

Collaboration with designers: Set, costume, lighting and music

Visiting the space

In the UK set and costumes are often designed by the same designer and that has generally been my experience.

Whenever possible I love visiting the theatre space with the designer, sitting in it, breathing in its atmosphere, walking the stage, getting a sense of how the space 'works'. What are its strengths, how can we build on them? What are its weaknesses, how can we compensate? Pondering together how best to use the space, its height, depth, and relationship to the audience.

Visiting the space is often a luxury and not always possible. For this reason a model box of the theatre becomes invaluable. The miniature model of the set made by the designer can be developed and tried out in that box. Of course, if you are designing for a tour there is the complication that the space is going to change with each venue. When touring with Shared Experience, making decisions for countless venues, our priority was to make sure the set would work well in its first performance space. From there, the touring solution was primarily about creating a set that would sit well almost anywhere – a tall order, but over the years I felt we became quite adept at creating sets that brought their own atmosphere with them. Whenever the opportunity arose it made me appreciate the luxury of designing for a single theatre space.

One of the biggest surprise shocks is walking into the theatre to see the built set for the very first time. I always do so with bated breath and a certain amount of fear. In almost every instance I find that everything looks huge, far bigger than I was imagining from the model box and the dimensions taped out in the rehearsal room. The initial shock can feel nightmarish. But I have gradually come to accept that the adage 'If it looks right in the model box, it will look right onstage' holds true. Once you have got over the shock of the size and you see actors walking about on the set, your brain can gradually adjust to the huge shift in scale. But if you were never sure about it in the model box, there is every chance you will be disappointed. This is no room for thinking 'I'm not sure about it, but it will probably look fine under the lights'.

In my experience there are two ways of approaching design. There are designers who are keen to offer ideas before any discussion with the director and those who prefer to find the set through collaboration. Both are valid approaches. In fact many directors would prefer a designer who will proactively initiate and suggest design.

Young designers new to the field might have recently completed a course in set design where they are often required to study a play and then come up with their own concept for set and costumes. Although they occasionally worked to a director's vision, more often it had to be their own. Excellent training, of course, but it is then quite a leap to work with a director who wants a close collaboration, whereby the director's concept guides the process from the start.

In every area of theatre, I find collaboration with others the most creative way to work – it feeds the imagination and takes one down unexpected avenues. In relation to set design, it means spending time together talking about the play and sharing the concept. At best this would mean a wide-ranging conversation with each of us, asking and answering questions about what that concept really means. Together we puzzle out a major consideration, what it is the set needs to express. Only once this has been defined does it make sense for the designer to go off on their own, do some work and bring back a few ideas to play with.

True collaboration

Katrina Lindsay is an inspired designer of set and costumes; we have worked together on many deeply satisfying collaborations. In Chapter 1, I described the search for a concept for *All's Well that Ends Well,* often considered one of Shakespeare's 'problem' plays. A particular challenge with this play is its fairy-tale world, where little feels real or consistent. Katrina and I had great difficulty finding a way to express this fairy-tale world. We would pore through her vast library of photographic books looking for inspiration, occasionally finding an image that we felt might connect to our material. A woman conceptual artist and photographer, Martha Rosler, had created powerful photographic composites of ordinary living rooms invaded by images of war; this was inspirational, a shocking mix of domesticity and war. And there was another book that we kept coming back to, a photographic record of a film inhabited by strange people in a hospital setting full of overgrown plants and weird equipment. I am not sure what Donald Sutherland and Geraldine Chaplin were doing in this film, but its surreal world became a powerful trigger for visual ideas for our fairy tale.

In fairy tales, we don't have to explain everything. This fairy-tale concept led to playful decisions. Helena and Bertram leave England and end up in a French court, so perhaps everyone in that French court could be dressed head to toe in white. Why not? In a fairy tale, anything goes. In addition it meant we need not be specific about national costume or military style. This was liberating. Helena has magical qualities and in the course of the play she cures the King of France of a serious disease. To enchance the magic, once she has miraculously cured him, we had her dress change colour from pale mauve in one scene to deep red in the next. I mention these details as examples of how a very tight concept can be so freeing. The concept guides the decisions. The old cliché: necessity is the mother of invention. Restriction can be counted on to provoke creativity.

Case study

Collaborating on adaptation and design for *Anna Karenina*

Here is an example of a collaboration that grew between the writer, the director and the designer.

The writer

Helen Edmundson's process for adaptation suited her as a writer, but I can imagine other writers might approach things differently. When we began investigating *Anna Karenina*, she and I spent time together discussing the book and our responses to it. The challenge lay in the novel dealing with two parallel stories – one about Anna and the other about the character of Levin, who in many ways was the essence of Tolstoy himself. Early on, Helen's aim was to define the major theme she would be developing. Possibilities were discussed:

- *A forbidden love* so obsessive and compulsive that it destroys the lovers' lives.
- *Fear of death*: Levin's struggle with his fear of death; Anna's defiance of death, leading her to pursue a love even though it might destroy her.

Before Helen began writing, we would have short workshops to explore physical solutions to images from the book. As examples, for *Anna Karenina* we explored visual images for society rejecting Anna the adulterer. And we improvised in movement, for example exploring Levin's dream/nightmare to see what would emerge. Later on, for *War and Peace,* with co-director Polly Teale, we workshopped ways of creating battles onstage. For *Mill on the Floss,* we explored adults playing children. Subsequently Helen would take time on her own to do the writing, meeting occasionally with the directors. Although this method worked for her as a writer, other writing approaches might be more involved with a continuous writer/company/director process in the rehearsal room.

Researching Anna Karenina

Before Helen began writing *Anna Karenina,* she and I made a week-long research trip to Moscow and St Petersburg. What an adventure! The USSR in October 1991 had only just come through a failed coup to overthrow President Gorbachev and his attempts at democratization. The economy was in freefall, and it was hard to find food that was palatable to our refined Western tastes. By December the Soviet Union would no longer exist.

At that time one could only visit Russia with an official group and Intourist Guide. We were advised by a friend to bring packaged cheese and crackers for sustenance along with cigarettes and biros for necessary bribes. We never once saw a sign written in English and our one attempt to travel alone in Moscow, on foot and underground, was frightening in its foreignness. It was a strange time to be there. But we were fortunate in that we came with introductions to fascinating theatre people and saw two deeply inspiring productions: *Crime and Punishment* and *The Taming of the Shrew.* In both productions we could not understand a word, but we agreed that the power of the actors' physical presence was astonishing. Their ability to express their inner states through their physicality was deeply engaging. Later we met with one of their directors and were overwhelmed when she explained that the power in their work came from 'a sense of mortality'.

Searching for a concept

During the trip Helen was pondering how to approach Tolstoy's great novel. On first reading it can come across as two completely different books. Anna's story and Levin's story have equal weight and yet these two characters meet only once. Through family connections and events, Tolstoy manages to artfully interweave their lives. Traditional adaptations concentrate on Anna and her rapturous and tragic love affair with Count Vronsky. But I had always loved Levin's journey and was keen to include both strands in our adaptation. Helen was not sure this would be possible.

Wherever we went we asked people about *Anna Karenina*. Everyone, it seemed, including guides and museum keepers, knew the book well. Helen would always ask them which story they preferred, that of Anna or that of Levin. Each time Helen asked, they would reply: 'Both.' For a Russian, it seemed, any version of *Anna Karenina* had to include both stories.

The night train from Moscow to St Petersburg

Halfway through our week, Helen and I were on the overnight train from Moscow to St Petersburg. We were replicating the exact journey made by Anna in the novel, as she returns home to her husband and young son in St Petersburg. In Moscow Anna had been to the ball where she met and danced with Count Vronsky, an event which was about to destroy her marriage and change her life forever.

As we sat together in our compartment, unable to sleep, we shared swigs from our trusty bottle of scotch and Helen revealed an idea she had that meant one could tell Anna's story and Levin's story in the same play. We would be watching scenes from Anna's life while Levin looked on from the edge of the stage. Suddenly when the character of Anna was feeling stressed she would speak to him, asking: 'Where are you now?' As he began to answer, we would enter scenes from his life. And later, when his life became difficult or lonely, Levin could just as suddenly say to the watching Anna: 'Where are you now?' which would take us back to Anna's story. Their stories would continue to unfold, moving back and forth between them.

To this day I marvel at this device. It was such a brilliant solution and at some point it led us to the idea that the play was taking place in Tolstoy's brain. It meant the Levin character could have an attitude to Anna's choices. He could warn her, advise her, attempt to save her from rash decisions. Tolstoy was a man tormented by an ambivalence in his own nature. I came to believe that if Levin represented one side of Tolstoy, then Anna represented the other side – the side that was ruled by his senses, the side that was out of control. Somehow Helen had found a theatrical device which took on board these warring aspects of Tolstoy's nature.

Designer's research

As we worked on Helen's adaptation, the designer Lucy Weller hit on what was to become an inspirational piece of research. She had discovered that Vladimir Nabokov, widely known as the author of *Lolita,* had a fascination with Tolstoy's novel and that his lecture notes on the book had been published. Nabokov was so taken with the sensual and symbolic physical elements described in Anna's overnight train journey from Moscow to St Petersburg that he had made a pencil drawing of the train carriage and all its elements. In his novel, Tolstoy describes the night, the howling blizzard outside, the end doors of the carriage which open suddenly, blowing in snow and cold air as conductors passed through the car, Anna's small red handbag – the same red bag she is carrying years later just before she jumps to her death in front of a train.

We were inspired by this material, and it took us on the next step of collaboration. As we had come to imagine the play was unfolding in Tolstoy's brain, that suggested an impressionistic world for the play. And now with this discovery of Nabokov's drawing of visual elements associated with travel, Lucy and I began to ponder doing the whole play with elements found in that railway carriage. We would limit our scenic elements to chairs, luggage and doors.

This was an idea that grew and grew. Lucy designed huge sliding doors to the rear of the space which could open and close suddenly and with great force. Every character entered and exited through those doors just as the conductors had in Anna's train carriage. Our only furniture was a set of bentwood chairs. When it snowed, the snow poured from a suitcase; when Levin worked his farm, he stood over a large open trunk shovelling grain.

Collaboration is energizing. It leads to unexpected solutions. Looking back I would be hard pressed to remember where the ideas originally came from. This collaboration between the writer and the designer had led the way to a minimalist, impressionistic design, a concept which invited the audience to imagine the world we were creating with just a few chosen elements: doors, luggage, chairs.

The working relationship

I mention open and wide-ranging conversation with the designer, but this does not always happen, nor is it easy to achieve. It needs time. If two strangers have come together in order to collaborate, one cannot assume a real ease and freedom to speak one's mind. I may admire the designer's work; I probably have studied their portfolio of previous productions and asked questions about how solutions were arrived at; I have been clear with them about my process and how I want to work in close collaboration from the start with someone who is on board to express my concept. But is it possible the first time you work with a designer to have real freedom and close collaboration? Maybe. In my experience the first project is always going to feel tentative. How sensitive is this person? Can I really speak my mind? Will they accept the moments when I reject an idea? Am I sensitive to them and their process so that they are creative even when we challenge each other? We will only be able to trust each other's judgement and taste when we have experienced an entire production process and come through the opening night with real respect for each other. No wonder people choose to work with the same artists again and again. The process is so much more comfortable and full of trust.

A lesson learnt

Steve came to an interview in my search for a designer for Brecht's *A Caucasian Chalk Circle*. I had already seen some of his work and found it quite brilliant. His idea was to produce the play as if it were a touring show being set up off the back of a truck, and in his interview he began sketching out ideas on paper. I was taken aback as I was looking for a collaborative experience and felt this was more than premature. Let's face it, the production would already be Steve's vision. He was not curious to hear my ideas, which I confess were still vague in my mind. However, it is also possible that Steve was bringing his ideas in so quickly because he wanted to make a good impression at this job interview.

Despite my respect for Steve's talent and what he would bring to the show, experience had taught me that I would not be able to function with him collaboratively. It brought back too many painful memories of my early directing days when I had gone along with a designer and what they were suggesting simply because the ideas were beautiful or clever and I could think of no good reason to reject what was being offered.

I had learned the hard way. Early on when I am about to a direct a play, my imagination starts to mull over a concept. And often an image or visual idea will come into my mind – literally pop into my head. I tend to think this is the area in the brain which produces images when we are dreaming, the creative non-censorious side. I would bring these vague thoughts to early design meetings, but was often waylaid by a designer who had a passion for a particular idea. It's not surprising that I was impressed by their offering. At this point my own ideas were still only vague hunches which needed examination and teasing out, whereas the designer was already making impressive sketches. And so I would be persuaded.

As rehearsals progressed it became painfully evident that I had not really connected with what the designer had proposed. I was unable to play or work with the elements in the set. I found myself harking back to my initial suggestions and impulses for the physical world. I missed those images, longed for them, and always regretted that I had let them go. We had missed out the vital step in the process when I could present a concept and have it lead the work. The designer's sketches might dazzle with their creativity, but finally they were arbitrary.

There are several issues here. If the designer is able to offer a complete idea as a starting point, surely this is a solution which they might have offered to any director producing the play. And I stress again, this is a perfectly valid process which many find fruitful. But my preference for collaboration means that ultimately the set will express my particular concept of what the play is about, what it wants to say. In the director/designer collaboration I need to share ideas, passion and concept so that they lead the design process.

The Cherry Orchard

When my husband David Aukin was artistic director of the Leicester Haymarket Theatre he invited John Byrne to be his resident head of design. Byrne is a hugely multitalented artist working as a painter, writer and theatre designer. In 1984 he was best known for his trilogy of plays *The Slab Boys*, and in future would write the award-winning television series *Tutti Frutti* and *Your Cheatin' Heart*. I was associate director at the Haymarket, about to direct Chekhov's *The Cherry Orchard* to be designed by John.

One day he brought me a stunning model he had already built for the production. It was a forest of trees wrapped in painted fabric which covered the entire stage. I was taken aback as we had not yet opened discussions. Looking back, I can only think that this passionate artist was satisfying an instinct to present his vision in real terms, rather than providing sketches or resorting to 'talk'. And although I could appreciate its beauty and power, I had to explain that I was not able to engage with this design. In particular I felt it would not allow for comedy, a major aspect of *The Cherry Orchard*; I needed the design to be a joint effort, a collaboration. John was understanding, so we started again from scratch, puzzling together possible design ideas. In the end the design solutions were a world away from that first forest, but every bit as powerful. And, most importantly, following our discussions the set now expressed my sense of what the play was about.

White card

Some years ago I travelled to Spain in order to visit the Guggenheim Museum in Bilbao, designed by the remarkable architect Frank Gehry. In an exhibition about his lengthy design process I learned that Gehry forbade his assistants to work on the building models in any material but white card, mainly because the cheap white card was easy to rip apart, crush, eliminate and change. Here was confirmation for my long-held instinct to ask designers to work initially only in white card.

When looking together at a set model, if one wonders aloud 'How would it look if you moved this bit or took it out?' the actual action of cutting into the model or ripping something apart is painful for both parties. But if everything is in cheap white card, it feels like an invitation to play with the elements, and keeps open any decisions to be made about colour. You don't want to use colour too soon as you might become attached to it before such decisions are necessary or creative.

Music and sound

Theatre composers often deal with both music and sound. I had the great good fortune early on when I met Peter Salem, a composer I have worked with for many years as a close collaborator. He has composed music and sound on most of my work for almost thirty years. Such a relationship has been fruitful because we understand each other and appreciate each other's values and taste. These things are hard to measure and even harder to explain. Suffice it to say that when it has been necessary for me to work with other composers and sound designers, it was always challenging, because we did not have the shorthand and understanding I had come to value with Peter.

When possible I spend time with the composer and sound person talking through my concept: what I hope to express with the piece, and what flavour I imagine for each piece of music or sound design. Ideally they will offer suggestions by way of samples that we can listen to together and discuss. In the best experience, the music and sound will come into the production gradually. This means having recordings or at least something on a phone that one can try out.

If you are having sound scoring which plays under the dialogue, it is excellent to have it in rehearsal so that everyone gets used to it. When the underscoring is brought in at the last minute, it can be disruptive and hard to adjust to. Once we are onstage, far too often I have found myself cutting an underscore because it felt distracting. But I query those decisions. If we had been able to have the underscoring earlier, perhaps it would have become an organic part of the scene.

Lighting

When there is a problem, we theatre people joke ruefully: 'Don't worry, it will look great under the lights.' I am not sure how long that expression has been around, but it is certainly true that stage lighting can be enhancing and transformative. Sometimes lighting a show can feel like having a secret superpower. With light one can create atmospheres, shadows and mystery. When light is directed specifically it can lead the spectator's eyes to a chosen place on the stage and then subtly move their gaze to wherever one might like. A doorway can become an area full of mystery or hope or even dread. A character's face, hidden in shadow, can be touched by a fine ray of light gently creeping in to reveal expression. A sky can gradually darken menacingly, or brighten joyously. Truly the lighting designer's magic paintbox is at your disposal, serving your vision for the play, its meaning, and what it wants to express.

I love the first moments of technical rehearsal where lighting is introduced – a time full of promise. Those moments feel crucial as you begin to sense how the designer's choices are transporting the space and the set into a new dimension. Taste in lighting is so subjective that it might take a while to arrive at a place of understanding with your lighting designer. And it is a particularly delicate time if you are working together for the first time. Given that technical hours are tight, there is an urgent need to communicate and sense each other out, without stepping on each other's toes. For me it is always a challenge to be patient and give time for this complex process.

How has the designer chosen to treat the space, to explore its special elements and dramatic possibilities? Sometimes I, as director, will suggest adding light to bring out different qualities in the set. This can mean taking precious time to mount or move lighting instruments so that areas which seem dead can come alive.

A stubborn pillar

For *A Midsummer Night's Dream* at the RSC, Katrina Lindsay, the set designer, and I had included a hefty white brick pillar which disappeared up into the fly tower. On a spare all-white set it added architectural interest and became very useful for characters to hide behind, climb up or emerge from. But I felt it was looking heavy, like a leaden, dead area in the midst of our playing space. Our lighting designer was happy to focus lights onto this pillar so that it glowed architecturally in various states of brightness as if lit from within, quickly becoming a live element in the space.

This might feel like an unnecessary and fiddly obsession with tiny details, but I do believe that every inch of the theatre picture is playing its part in telling the story, exactly as it would in a painting. And that everything on the set should only be there for a reason, because it has a role to play.

8

Discovering physical theatre

In the late 1960s physical theatre entered our lives. After a year studying classical acting in London I had returned to the States. As the off-off-Broadway movement was emerging, several alternative, experimental theatre companies were making their mark. Peter Schumann's Bread and Puppet Theater had begun in 1963; Julian Beck and Judith Malina's company, the Living Theatre, had just returned from several years abroad with their hugely influential productions including *Frankenstein* and *Paradise Now*; Joseph Chaikin had broken away from the Living Theatre to form the Open Theater; Ellen Stewart, founder of La MaMa E.T.C. (Experimental Theatre Club), was sponsoring the work of Tom O'Horgan, who went on to restage the hugely successful *Hair* on Broadway. These avant-garde companies were intent on experiment and exploring physical theatre techniques. A main influence was Antonin Artaud's Theatre of Cruelty (*Le Théâtre et son double*, 1938) and techniques that had come from Poland (Jerzy Grotowski's *Towards a Poor Theatre*, 1968). An example of their influence comes across in this wikipedia quote from the Living Theatre's Julian Beck: 'To involve or touch or engage the audience, not just show them something.'

La MaMa Plexus

In 1968, fortunately for me a new physical experimental company was starting up in New York, supported by Ellen Stewart's Café La MaMa, and as I previously mentioned in my introduction, they were welcoming anyone keen to learn and explore. We became known as La MaMa Plexus, an unpaid company directed by Stanley Rosenberg. Stanley had been interning in Denmark at Odin Theater with Eugenio Barba, a disciple of Poland's hugely influential Grotowski. By now I had left acting behind but was able to join the company as an assistant director with the understanding that my first commitment would be to experience the work fully by joining in all the acting exercises.

We met in the late afternoons, which meant we could do teaching jobs or, in my case, continue study for a Master's degree in performance theory at New York University. The work was arduous, using physical training exercises, sound and movement games, some yoga, a great deal of slow-motion improvisation. Having previously studied acting by following Stanislavski's practices and mental, thought-led exercises, here was an alternative realm. We were starting with the physical, the actor's body and imagination were at the centre of the work. Develop the actor's creativity and physical expression to its limits. Start from there.

As our leader Stanley Rosenberg offered little explanation about what we were doing and why we were doing it, the experience became quite mysterious, what I imagined to be a zen experience. The work did have a philosophy behind it, influenced by Artaud's book *Le Théâtre et son double/The Theatre and Its Double*, his manifesto for a Theatre of Cruelty. Because we performed the exercises without question, the work felt daring and liberating. After all this was the 1960s, hence a desire to throw yourself into something new in a non-censorious spirit. We were in our twenties and living in the days of flower power, pot smoking, LSD, bra burning, anti-Vietnam war marches and communal living. Anything experimental was embraced.

The sessions would end with extended, slow-motion physical improvisation to music. As time went by, the atmosphere in the room became potent. Moving in slow motion is not only freeing, but can also be intensely satisfying and hypnotic. The music and interaction with others inspired the movement. No words were spoken. It felt increasingly as though we were travelling through an extraordinary dream without a need for meaning or effect. Meeting other bodies and interacting with them we became more expressive, liberated; we were probably moving towards dance, certainly not naturalism. It was a trip.

This work puts the actor at the centre, the actor's physical and psychic presence fills the space powerfully. In production terms it meant stripping away all artifice. Just enough stage lighting to see. Music and sound made by the actors. Set and costumes kept to the barest essentials.

This introduction to working from the body, physically, intuitively was revelatory. I felt freer than I ever had in a traditional rehearsal room or class. Through this purely physical approach, I think we were getting in touch with the creative side of our brain, from my understanding, the side which intuits, imagines and is non-judgemental. The results were thrilling. I watched actors exploring scenes from Greek tragedy using these physical theatre exercises. Language was added in by an actor on the side speaking the lines aloud, giving out the text one sentence at a time. We also spoke in slow-motion speech. As one had no idea what the next line was, one could remain completely and totally in the moment. Time was stretched and movement became an expressionistic exploration of how the words and situation were affecting you.

From this time onward I became a devotee of starting with the physical whenever possible. But that sort of work needs time and space in rehearsal when you can introduce exercises and train a company together. It requires like-minded people who are open to exploration. Only then can you begin to look at whole scenes without using words and open the way to expressionistic work. By 'expressionistic' I mean work that expresses the inner, often hidden life of the characters, their hopes, fears, aspirations and dreams.

A great deal of my theatre work continued in a traditional environment where these discoveries could only be touched on, but I was able to pursue these exercises and techniques with Freehold (1968–73), the Leicester Haymarket Studio Company (1984–6) and Shared Experience (1989–2011).

An inspiring teacher

In the early 1990s, when I had already been directing for some twenty years, I travelled to the Edinburgh Festival on a quest. I had recently been appointed the new artistic director of Shared Experience. The Edinburgh Festival was a famed hotbed of new writing, invention and radical experiment. When I arrived in the city I wanted to be surprised and said to my friends: 'I want to see some theatre that changes my idea of what theatre is or can be.' I struck lucky. My quest led me to a show called *Tattoo* which was making a huge impact. Directed by Mladen Materic of Sarajevo, the piece had created such a stir that an extra performance was hurriedly arranged for a midnight showing. Thankfully I was able to get a ticket and sat rapt at midnight while the work unfolded before me. *Tattoo* did not disappoint. It was a startling experience, a play enacted entirely without words, and yet it bore no resemblance to mime as I knew it. The characters were behaving in a realistic manner. As their lives passed before me, their story was being told exclusively through body language, position in space and specific use of props. Even now find I find it impossible to describe the effect in more detail – it simply had to be seen.

This performance was to influence my whole way of working. Previously I had few exercises that would open a company to working so fully through the body, using the body as a starting point. My only method would be to recreate the hypnotic, slow-motion exploration of my La MaMa Plexus days. But this required unrealistically long and extensive rehearsal periods. In discovering Mladen Materic I had finally come across a training method which could take a group into physical work quickly and organically.

Fortuitously Materic was in Edinburgh with *Tattoo* and I invited him to London to run workshops. His exercises were an education and an inspiration. As with any good exercises, I was keen to try them out myself and gradually develop them in ways that worked for me. The chair exercise I use to explore wants (see Chapter 3) developed from one of these exercises.

9

Working in different mediums

Physical theatre and film

In 1989 when I became artistic director of Shared Experience Theatre I made a commitment to expressionistic work. Through our physical work we would act out the characters' hidden thoughts, dreams, fears and desires. I chose material which invited this approach. We produced adaptations of nineteenth-century novels which lent themselves to expressionism. Women in those works, such as Anna in *Anna Karenina* and Maggie Tulliver in *Mill on the Floss*, led lives of extreme repression. Their inner, hidden lives cried out for expression.

As a theatre director I was keen to tell the story through the visual elements, the set, the lighting and character positions in space. We can understand a huge amount about people and their emotional lives through body language: the way they enter a room, the way they handle props, the distance they keep between themselves and others. When working in theatre, my hope was that even an audience that spoke no English could get a strong sense of what was happening simply through the physical relationships and how they shifted as the story was being told. This proved to be an invaluable link to film.

Directing a first film

I first met Wendy Kesselman in 1987 when I was invited by the feminist theatre company Monstrous Regiment to direct the UK premiere of her play *My Sister in This House*. Working together was extremely satisfying, which meant it was a great opportunity when we found ourselves working on the screen adaptation for the Oscar-winning film producer Norma Heyman. Wendy was impressively open and knowledgeable about film and therefore more than capable of adapting her stage play to this medium.

Directing a film felt like a gift. In theatre the director spends a great deal of time and effort trying to direct the audience's focus. The playing space is large. The actor is small. How do I get the audience to focus where I want them to? Where do I want their eyes to go at each moment? Lighting becomes hugely important and can direct the spectator's eye from one moment to the next, specific focus can be achieved. But in film that focus becomes a thousandfold more possible. In the medium of cinema I could obsess even more about the pictures and the story they were telling. Choosing where to place the camera became a great adventure, a brilliant tool for how I desired the audience to experience the moment.

Fast learning curve

I should add that the cliché 'ignorance is bliss' comes into its own when you are a first-time film director. You have little idea of usual practice and no sense that you might be breaking rules. On my first film *Sister My Sister*, I was so busy learning that I had little time to doubt myself.

I have made only two feature films, *Sister My Sister* (1994) and *Alive and Kicking* (1996) (originally known as *Indian Summer*), so my understanding of this will be limited, but here is the bottom line as I see it. At heart, a film crew wants a leader, someone at the helm who has a vision. In fact the film marketing magazines often refer to the director as the 'helmer', with all its connotations of steering a very large ship. Most importantly the designers and crew want to work on a film where the leader has a vision they have a passion to fulfil. If it comes across that you indeed have a vision, that you have a sense of what you are trying to achieve in each shot or scene or performance, they will follow you with avid dedication.

For a theatre director this enthusiasm can be hugely refreshing. In theatre the participants – and by this I mean designers, actors and technical staff – are in a position to evaluate the project as it is growing and evolving. They have a sense of 'how it is going', whether certain performances are coming on well. This can feel judgemental. The actors may be protective of their careers and will pull against the director if they do not have total trust. The technical crew may not be 100 per cent behind every whim or idea proposed by the director. 'Do we really need that metal cage to descend slowly from the flies with two actors in it?' 'Are you spending too much time working on that sequence?' 'Will all this drumming become an irritant?' In short, the director may feel doubt about their abilities and taste creeping into the rehearsal room.

How unexpected and surprising then to discover that the culture of film is so different. Many working on a film set suspect that they may never see the finished product. Yes, they will be invited to the 'cast and crew' screening of the film, but this is probably months away and it is likely many of them will be busy on other film sets by then and not free to attend. I assume this distance from the finished film explains why the concentration is focused so sharply on each day's shooting and achieving the footage that will finally be edited into a finished product. In short, those working day-to-day on set are passionately dedicated to satisfying every whim of the leader, the vision person.

To my delight, the atmosphere on set was hugely intoxicating. Large numbers of people all waiting to please me. Everyone wanting to know what I think. Where do I want the camera? Do I like the flowers, the wallpaper, the costume, the makeup?

Do I want to do countless takes of the scene until I feel it is right? If something is not as I had hoped, can it be changed? Just say it, they will try to make it happen. It was a far cry from theatre and the rehearsal rooms and technical sessions I had experienced.

Preparation

Of course there was a lot of preparation before we got to the first day of shooting. I did need help and was lucky to come across *Making Movies*, a book by the brilliant Sidney Lumet. His movies had always been inspiring: *Dog Day Afternoon*, *Twelve Angry Men*, *Network*, to name a few. In his excellent handbook, Lumet describes every aspect of film making with great clarity without relying on academic knowledge. I would recommend it to any first-time film director.

Because my producer, Norma Heyman, wanted to protect me, she was keen for me to have a camera operator who was also the cinematographer. This protection was invaluable as it meant I was collaborating with just one person about camera position and camera lighting. Had I been getting suggestions from two separate experts it could have been overwhelming for a novice. I would recommend this to any new director.

I also visited a few film sets so that I could soak up the atmosphere and get a sense of standard procedure and be prepared for the large numbers of people at work on a busy set. Ken Loach was enormously welcoming. And finally I got invaluable help from the fine film director Mike Leigh, whom I knew from my theatre work. One Sunday I rang him for advice and he taught me (over the phone) how to prepare a provisional list of shots for each day, with simple drawings. This meant I arrived on set each morning with a plan for discussion.

Before I began filming, I watched several films which I admired and I became concerned about camera movement. I could see the camera travelling, but the more films I watched the more insecure I felt about that language and how it worked.

Even if I were to dip into textbooks, given that I was on a crash learning course, how could I take on this new language? I was rescued by the great Ingmar Bergman, director of so many inspirational films, including the brilliant *Fanny and Alexander*. I learnt that Bergman often used a stationary camera and would hold shots for unusually long takes. He was intent on exploring and capturing the inner lives of his characters, keeping the camera in tight close-up on their faces.

I had to assume that my main strength in making a film would be how I direct the actors and nurture their performances. Clearly I was not a novice in that realm, so I took my cue from Bergman. When I met potential cinematographers/camera operators I cited Bergman and explained that I wanted to keep the camera still and concentrate on capturing performance. Years later I discovered that Bergman in fact also used panning shots and zoom, but at the time my desire to keep the camera still worked in my favour. *Sister My Sister* was a tense psychological drama and the stillness of the camera, masterly deployed by Ashley Rowe cinematographer, added to the tension.

As soon as I began working on set, things seemed to fall into place. My work preparing the script with the writer and developing ideas with the set designer meant that my head was full of visual ideas of how to tell the story. And directing actors was more than familiar – hence my entry into a new medium felt exciting and adventurous.

Alive and Kicking: A close relationship

The relationship between the camera operator and the director can be a deeply satisfying collaboration. On my second film *Alive and Kicking,* written by Martin Sherman, I worked closely with cinematographer/camera operator Chris Seager. We would talk about the scene and the feeling or atmosphere I had in mind. I would suggest where to put the camera for the shot which takes in the whole scene: the wide shot. Chris would work with my choice, lighting the space and setting up the camera. We would then move on to less wide shots and to close-ups.

When Seager was filming, looking through the camera, he explained to me that he could tell if the actor was performing truthfully because he would be unable to take his eye from the actor's face. But if, while the camera rolled, his eye wandered around the image taking in details of lighting or framing, then he sensed that this was not a good 'take', that the actor was not totally inside the character. He would quietly let me know his opinion. As director it was then up to me whether we rolled the camera again for another take. It was gratifying to feel one was in a partnership and that another practised eye was there to help.

Editing

To discover the world of film editing can feel a bit like Alice going through the looking glass. For me it opened a door into a unique realm of creative possibility. I feel fortunate that the two films I directed, *Sister My Sister* and *Alive and Kicking*, were edited in an entirely traditional way. Both films were produced by Film4, which at that time required films to be edited without the help of the emerging new digital technology.

I am grateful to have had the more traditional experience, a painstakingly slow process where it could take an entire morning for the editor to re-cut a scene in order to change its tone or storytelling. This meant a great deal of thought and collaborative conversation between editor and director before such a change was scheduled. And if a viewing of the newly cut scene felt like a mistake, it could take another morning to put it back to its original form or perhaps aim for a third version. By contrast, using present-day technology, a scene can be manipulated, played with and tried out in myriad ways practically at an instant. Naturally it means that film editing is now a completely different experience.

Whatever the technology, editing remains a deeply creative craft that gives the director great power. An actor may have been asked to play a scene in several different ways, e.g. angry, hesitant, repressed, and because the director has that choice of performances on film or tape, they can choose to put moments together and shape a performance which never existed at the time. If we found an actor was not powerful enough in a scene, we might find bits of their performance from another version of the scene which would give us the quality we needed. As editing consists of pasting together a scene moment by moment, the possibilities of altering performance are great. Many actors find it difficult to watch themselves in a film as they may be seeing a performance created not by them, but by the director combining different versions of the scene.

When filming is complete, the editor is given time to do an 'assembly'. Using the raw material of scenes that have been shot, they assemble the film in a way which makes sense to them. One can expect an assembly to be quite long as the editor does not want to take too many liberties with the material, but my first view of the assembly for *Sister My Sister* was a huge shock. The film is about two sisters locked in a destructive relationship. In my mind the film was being told from the point of view of Christine, the older dominant sister. However the editor had made assumptions and had assembled the material in such a way that the story was told from the point of view of the younger sister, Lea. I was astonished and concerned, but soon learned that with the magic of editing the relationship and point of view I had imagined were easily restored.

Because every decision to try something new with a scene, or even the order of scenes, would become so time-consuming, there were many intense conversations between the editor, his assistant and myself. Personally I found this time creative and collaborative. In contrast, the few experiences I have had of editing digitally are very different. All eyes in the editing suite are on the screens you are working on and changes can be made instantly. This new technology has no doubt had a profound effect on film making, but I shall always feel privileged to have had that more traditional experience.

Musical score

Learning about musical and sound score in film is an extraordinary and compelling journey. I found myself watching films that I admired while obsessively following their use of sound and placement of music cues. It is an area I found fascinating as I gradually came to believe that the best scores are those of which we are least aware. They work on us subliminally and yet their effect is powerful and transporting. I find that when I am overly aware of the score while I am watching a film, it can be disruptive rather than enhancing.

Music can affect our emotions so profoundly that the score for a film becomes an extremely powerful element. Music will create the tone for the film and finding a tone that works for both the composer and the director can be a delicate balance. Finally the music needs to serve the director's vision. If the music is very emotional, effectively telling the audience what to feel, it can have completely the opposite effect.

During the edit most directors work with a 'temp track', using already existing music often from other films, to underscore. This can be an inspiring way to work, but the danger is one can become overly attached to that music for which the rights are not available. It then becomes a challenge for your composer to replace that temp track with a score that is original and also achieves the desired tone.

While editing *Alive and Kicking*, Martin Sherman's film about a dancer, for an extended dance sequence we used a Vivaldi track. It worked brilliantly for the editing and it was a tall order for composer Peter Salem to create a new score to replace the Vivaldi. But, thankfully, he succeeded.

Ballet

My theatre work unexpectedly opened another door and brought me into the world of ballet. Ashley Page was artistic director of Scottish Ballet when he saw the Shared Experience production of *Mill on the Floss* at the Kennedy Center in Washington DC, which I had co-directed with Polly Teale in collaboration with choreographer Liz Ranken. In this work, full of expressionistic movement sequences, Page saw a language he thought might work for ballet and he decided to commission a ballet to be created and directed by a theatre director in collaboration with a choreographer.

Page introduced me to choreographer Annabelle Lopez Ochoa. Based in Amsterdam, Annabelle would be embarking on her first full-length story ballet and she was happy to be on board with this experiment. I was to be the lead creative, overseeing the vision of the ballet while she would create the choreography – needless to say a huge component in the work. Before we began, I asked Annabelle to think carefully about whether she could accept this relationship. After all, as choreographer she would be accustomed to being fully in charge, making all decisions about story, scenery, lighting and costume. She was up for this venture, and so we set off on what became a remarkable journey.

I suggested several ideas, and we agreed finally on Tennessee Williams's great play *A Streetcar Named Desire*. As we were working together for the first time I wanted to bring a lot of possible imagery to the table. I needed to spend time on my own free associating, going through the play script and noting down any images which came to mind with the particular task of asking myself, how do we do this scene without words? Otherwise I would be in a position where I would mostly be responding to Annabelle's choreography and looking after the story telling. But if I was committed to this being my vision I needed to prepare, to get inside the script and let my mind play and explore images.

Luckily for me I was on a remote beach holiday, which was perfect for hours under an umbrella reading *A Streetcar Named Desire* and allowing my mind to bring up pictures and possibilities for expressing events in pure movement. During those hours I began to explore the idea of enacting the back story of Blanche DuBois. In Williams's play her history is revealed only gradually, but here was an opportunity through dance to express the tragic events of her youth.

In London, Annabelle and I arranged to spend one week together coming up with a scene-by-scene scenario. We spent our evenings at the theatre, seeking out work which was experimenting with form. Looking back I can only wonder at this new working relationship, and here luck surely played a part as we discovered our taste was similar. Our approach to story telling was minimalist and included imaginative use of props and scenic elements. We soon agreed to start the ballet with Blanche's back story – a decision which invited the audience to experience the ballet from her point of view.

Occasionally I would suggest a scene which was mentioned in the play but did not actually occur onstage and we agreed that I would have a session with the dancers to see if there were staging opportunities. An example was a scene in a bowling alley where the main character Stanley Kowalski could be introduced, showing off in front of his friends, being frustrated when he loses at bowling, getting into a fight. I imagined this as a purely physical way of introducing his character, his needs, his values and his importance in his world.

By the end of the week we had put together a scenario of twenty-three scenes. Of course we had Williams's play structure as our base – a gift for the story telling.

Workshop

During an early workshop at the Tramway, the home of Scottish Ballet in Glasgow, Annabelle would teach short duets to help us in casting the main roles of Stanley Kowalski, Blanche DuBois and her sister Stella. (We needed two or three dancers for each character who would play the roles on tour or in case of injury.) In addition, I introduced non-verbal acting exercises with chairs which explored playing a want and an obstacle. The dancers were impressively open to these exercises, taking the concepts on board very quickly. And because of their training, they were brilliant at retaining information. I also sketched in short scenes from the scenario which could tell the story in pure movement and gesture.

An example of want and obstacle

Stanley Kowalski has angered a local shopkeeper who threatens to cut off their credit. Stanley and his wife Stella cannot afford this.

Stella
Want: *To get Stanley to apologize to the shopkeeper*
Obstacle: *Fears his physical anger*

Stanley
Want: *To refuse to apologize*
Obstacle: *Fears losing Stella's love*

These exercises helped us to identify which dancers had real potential to be honest and engaging when acting was called for.

Rehearsals

In rehearsal Annabelle began choreographing scenes and I would observe, but I soon learned that she needed to be on her own for these early sketches and so I would come in later and share my thoughts on the story telling and characterization, often taking dancers aside to direct the acting.

Concept and vision

I am often asked how it was possible for a director and a choreographer to work together on a piece, given that choreography is the primary element in ballet. As agreed, this was to be an experiment with a director at the helm. I, as director, took overall responsibility for the concept and vision. Therefore initially I worked with designers whose work I admired: Niki Turner for set and costume, and Tim Mitchell for lighting. At each step of the way the designs were run past Annabelle for comment, suggestions and approval.

As for the music, I introduced Annabelle to composer Peter Salem, who had created scores for so much of my work in theatre and film. In terms of concept and vision it arose naturally that Annabelle, as choreographer, would oversee the music. Fortuitously she connected to Peter's work and was keen to have him on board. In fact, Peter Salem is now her living composer of choice, and they have gone on to create many ballets together – notably *Broken Wings* for English National Ballet, *Frida* for Dutch National Ballet, and *Doña Perón* for Ballet Hispánico in New York.

As the ballet came together and we would run sections, we became aware of gaps in the emotional through line. For example, there came a moment when Blanche feels totally destroyed, at a loss because Mitch, who was her only hope for marriage and a future, has discovered her lies and has rejected her. We needed a passage of time which allowed us into Blanche's inner state. I suggested we repeat the image that started the piece where Blanche is a delicate moth reaching desperately for the lightbulb overhead which might destroy her. As we went into that image, five women dancers emerged slowly on pointe from both wings, drifting towards her, a floating chorus of wounded, desolate moths all reaching for the light, expressing her desolation. Here was a moment when Annabelle and I were finding the choreographic expression together.

This unusual, perhaps unique experiment where a theatre director leads the project was a great adventure. Scottish Ballet had a major success with the ballet, winning awards, visiting Sadler's Wells Theatre twice and touring the US several times. But it is a model which does not fit easily into the working methods of the ballet world. Instead I have been able to work with Annabelle over the years as her dramaturg and artistic collaborator, relationships more understandable and financially possible for producing companies.

Epilogue

My motivation for writing this book came from a desire to pass on the tools and techniques I have learned or devised for bringing a play to life so that it exists on its own in time and space. As theatre is such a collaborative art involving so many people and elements, any production of a play is going to be a unique manifestation. Change one actor in one main role and the piece will be different. Change the design or the sound or the lighting and it becomes a different experience. Change the director and every aspect of the play will be different.

My priority as a director has always been to serve a story, ideally one which takes me on a voyage of discovery, a voyage that becomes a journey of the mind and the heart for an audience.

Finally it is my wish that these 'notes' might guide, inspire, or lead to questions that open doors.

ACKNOWLEDGEMENTS

I want to acknowledge people who influenced and encouraged me to believe I could make my way as a theatre director; at Antioch College in the sixties two inspiring teacher/directors Meredith Dallas (Dal) and Paul Treichler; at the Herbert Berghof Studios in New York City, Aaron Frankel and Bill Hickey, acting teachers who kick started me into moments of revelation that taught me what it meant to 'act'; my inspiring first agent the late Clive Goodwin and Jenne Casarotto the agent who faithfully followed me and my work to all corners of the UK; and last but not least the director Michael Rudman who supported me throughout my career, believing when few did, that women could direct plays.

In later years director and teacher Mladen Materic welcomed me into his rehearsal room where I learned so much about releasing actors into their bodies.

Polly Teale my co-artistic director at Shared Experience and choreographer Liz Ranken, with whom I collaborated in countless Shared Experience rehearsal rooms, enriched my working vocabulary beyond measure.

Once I began writing I was encouraged and cheered on by good friends who read chapters and gave invaluable feedback: Roger Graef, Patrick Sandford, Patricia Vandenberg, Annabel Leventon, Martin Sherman, Helen Edmundson, and John Lahr. Thanks also to my present agent Helen Mumby who had faith right from the start, reading the manuscript in several versions, and Anna Brewer, my editor at Bloomsbury Methuen, who advised and inspired.

I also need to thank the hundreds of actors I have worked with who explored with me and allowed me to learn on the job. Thanks are also due to the mother's helps who looked after my children during those intense days and nights of rehearsal. I am immensely grateful to my dear sons Daniel and Jethro who were such good sports about my crazy working hours and had to share their mother with a passion that meant she was often at the dinner table in a dream state.

And to David Aukin, my husband and work companion through the process of writing this book. David, you know I would not have got to this point without your support, your incisive advice and your unshakeable belief.

INDEX